CW00482209

Tynemouth
Remembered

by Charlie Steel

Previous page: Front Street, Tynemouth, c. 1920.

This book is dedicated to
Chris Lambert and Ken Banks
Fondly remembered

Copyright Charlie Steel 2014

First published in 2014 by

Summerhill Books
PO Box 1210, Newcastle-upon-Tyne NE99 4AH

www.summerhillbooks.co.uk

email: summerhillbooks@yahoo.co.uk

ISBN: 978-1-906721-77-0

No part of this publication may be reproduced, stored in a mechanical retrieval system, or transmitted, in any form or by any means, electronic, mechanical, photocopying, recording or otherwise, without prior permission of the author.

CONTENTS

Preface   3

Acknowledgements & Contributors   4

Introduction   5

Origins of Tynemouth   6

Borough of Tynemouth Coat of Arms   8

Folklore   11

The Coast and River   19

Streets & Places   30

Buildings   50

Churches & Cemeteries   66

The Railway   70

People   75

Organisations & Leisure   82

PREFACE

As I have mentioned in my previous books, local history research can often prove quite complex, because it involves seeking out many different sources to procure the required information and it is quite common for drawbacks to occur whenever a conflict of information is encountered. There are often many variations in historical accounts and records such as the spelling of words, names and places etc, and likewise dates can also conflict unless firm evidence exists to make them indisputable. Sometimes it simply requires logical interpretation combined with a little calculated judgement to process and simplify that information to make it easily understood. Because of this, it is therefore important to remember that any material or information can only be as reliable as the source from which it was obtained and there can never be any guarantee that everything is 100% accurate. With that in mind, I have researched the information contained in this publication to the best of my ability, and have attempted to ensure its accuracy as far as possible, however I am well aware that there will always be some details which are open to debate, especially those which may not be fully documented. If any obvious inaccuracies or omissions are found, it would be advantageous to advise me along with a provable reference source rather than being over-critical of the content, and this way with your help, they can be corrected for the benefit of any future editions.

Charlie Steel
March 2014

ACKNOWLEDGEMENTS & CONTRIBUTORS

It is not possible to put a book together of this nature without the assistance of others. The people listed below have each made a significant contribution and I consider that it is important to make a personal acknowledgement by name:

ITEM	CONTRIBUTOR
Grand Hotel	Eddie & Tina Hastie, Chris Davidge and Leonard McManus
Lion's Head Fountain	Tony Kerr
Percy Gardens	Ken Day
Policing in Tynemouth, Constables' Courage & the Tynemouth Coat of Arms	Ken Banks
Priory Motor Coach Co.	Stuart Lee
Tynemouth Volunteer Life Brigade	Chris Lambert, Peter Lilley, Will Hogg (Jnr)
Tynemouth Lifeboat	Adrian Don, Chris Lambert
Tynemouth Priory Theatre	Ray Lowry
Tynemouth Stations	Alan Young, Ylana First, Elaine Cusack, Gill Tiffin
Spital Dene & St Leonard's Hospital	Mike Coates

Special thanks also go to Carol and Mark Robinson (Roundabout Publications), Joyce Marti and Diane Leggett (North Tyneside Local Studies Library), Andrew Clark (Summerhill Books) as well as the following organisations:

Friends of Tynemouth Station
Ringston's Ltd
Tynemouth Golf Club

Percy Park Rugby Football Club
Tynemouth Amateur Swimming Club
Tynemouth Rowing Club

SOURCES OF REFERENCE:

Many reference sources and publications have also been utilised in order to complete this publication, however some of the more significant ones include the following:

Ordnance Survey Mapping	
North Shields Library – Local Studies Centre	
Northumberland Archives	
Remembering the Past Resourcing the Future	Kath Smith and contributors to the North Shields Library Club
Offbeat – Memories of Tynemouth Borough Police	Ken Banks
The Northumbrian Pub	Lynn F. Pearson
The Story of Northumberland Park	Mike N. Coates
Wards Directories	R. Ward & Sons
Tynemouth Village Conservation Area Character Appraisal	North Tyneside Council
Tynemouth & District Transport Company History	PSV Circle
Tynemouth Golf Club Ltd.	J. Bates
Wikipedia	Internet Based
Illustrated Guide to the Borough of Tynemouth 1900	

FURTHER READING:

North Shields Public Houses, Inns & Taverns Part One

North Shields Public Houses, Inns & Taverns Part Two –
Including Tynemouth, Cullercoats Whitley Bay & District

INTRODUCTION

This book was compiled to bring together under one volume, a collection of those articles which I have written since 2009 for the local monthly advertising publication, *Roundabout Tynemouth*. In many cases, the articles here have been extended to include additional text, photographs and pictures. The book is not intended to present an intensive or comprehensive history, but instead has been compiled to give the reader a general overview of Tynemouth and those aspects which may be deemed to be of general local and historical interest.

Tynemouth is situated on the North East coast of England at the entrance to the River Tyne. It was once part of a violent and turbulent kingdom, but now in the quietude of what was once a part of Northumberland, it is a beautiful village steeped in history and for centuries, has inspired writers, poets, artists, photographers and historians.

The ruins of the famous Castle and Priory sit on the headland, dominating Benebal Crag. The piers guard the entrance to the River Tyne and the imposing statue of Lord Cuthbert Collingwood looks out to sea with an ever watchful eye. The Long Sands have attracted holidaymakers and visitors since the 1800s, King Edward's Bay and The Haven were places of peace and tranquillity, and continue to remain so.

The entrance to the River Tyne itself affords some beautiful views; however a dark shadow lies beside the nearby Black Middens, which over the years have taken a grim toll on numerous ships and have claimed the lives of many mariners and rescuers.

Today, Tynemouth still retains much of its history. It is now a conservation area and although the village has undergone many changes, these have been sympathetically moderated in an effort to maintain its traditional warmth and character. I hope the collection in this book helps to tell a few stories and bring back a few memories of what used to be.

Charlie Steel
March 2014

Rington's Tea Distribution Depot, Hotspur Street, Tynemouth, c. 1940. The building was demolished and replaced by new apartments which adopted the name from this depot to become 'Rington Court', which is situated close to the corner of Percy Street.

ORIGINS OF TYNEMOUTH

The early history of Tynemouth is very long and complex, but its origins probably began when the Priory and Castle were built high on the cliffs overlooking the North Sea. This steep rocky headland is known as Benebal Crag, or Pen-bal Crag, of which the literary translation is: *'The head of the rampart on the rock.'* The actual Priory was founded around 617 AD, perhaps by Edwin of Northumbria and the monastery continued throughout the 9th and 10th centuries before being abandoned in 1008 AD. Plans to re-found the monastery were delayed during the Norman invasion, however by 1083, it came under the control of the monks of Jarrow, later passing in 1090 to the Benedictine House of St Alban's when the monks of that order began to arrive at Tynemouth. It is believed that in 1095 there was a castle on the site consisting of earthen ramparts and a wooden stockade, and by 1296 the prior of Tynemouth was granted royal permission to surround the monastery with walls of stone and in 1390 a gatehouse and barbican were added on the landward side of the castle. Over the centuries both the Priory and the Castle have been used as landmarks and served as important fortifications against the Vikings, Scots and the armies of Napoleon.

On the whole, the Vikings who invaded Tynemouth and other parts of the North East coast were raiders rather than settlers. Evidence suggests that Viking settlement on the North Eastern coast of England was confined mainly to Yorkshire, south of the River Tees.

The coat of arms for the Prior of Tynemouth was a red shield with three crowns commemorating the tradition that the Priory had been the burial place for three kings that were buried there.

In 651, Oswin, King of Deira was murdered, and subsequently his body was brought here for internment. He became St Oswin and his burial place became a shrine visited by pilgrims. He was the first of the three kings buried at Tynemouth. In 792, Osred who had been king of Northumbria from 789 to 790 and then deposed was murdered. He was the second King to be buried at Tynemouth Priory. In 1093, Malcolm III of Scotland invaded England and was killed at Alnwick by Robert de Mowbray. Malcolm's body was buried at Tynemouth Priory for a time, but it is believed that he was subsequently re-buried in Dunfermline, in Scotland.

During both world wars the castle was used as a coastal defence and the restored magazines of the gun battery can still be seen. Nowadays much of the priory church remains, though most of the domestic outbuildings of the monastery have disappeared.

Tynemouth Priory in 1450.

For centuries, the actual village of Tynemouth basically consisted of the present Front Street, which led to the castle gate, and the subsidiary Back Street and Percy Street. Fields and lands to the north of the village were part of the Manor of Tynemouth, owned by the Duke of Northumberland which in 1868 was laid out for much of the present housing, where many of the street names have family associations. (Percy Street/Percy Park/Percy Gardens, Hotspur Street, Warkworth Terrace, Syon Street etc). During the 19th century, the coming of the railway contributed to the growth and expansion of the village, and in 1839 the first station opened at Oxford Street. This was superseded in 1882 by the magnificent glass-roofed structure towards the west side of the village, when the North Tyne loop came into being, bringing with it much of the tourist trade. This new Victorian railway station welcomed everyone with impressive displays of potted plants arranged around the platforms, and flower baskets hanging from the beams. The popularity of the railway soon became a gateway, bringing thousands of visitors into Tynemouth during the summer months to embrace the sea air. Priors Haven, sheltered and flanked on three sides by high banks, soon became a popular centre for the new fashion of sea bathing, which in Victorian days was always considered a cure for various ailments. Further north, waters off the Long Sands were reputed to have tonic qualities, and by the early 1900s the beach housed dozens of bathing machines, fairground and donkey rides, souvenir and food stalls. At certain times of the year, the beach could be packed with huge crowds.

Much of Tynemouth's development dates to Victorian days, and the Aquarium and Palace dominated the cliff tops above the long sands from 1878. Tynemouth Park which opened in 1893, stood directly opposite. The park was laid out as the village recreation park and incorporated a large boating lake, gardens and bowling greens.

Beaconsfield House stood a little further to the north, and was the mansion of a Mr John Burn, a coal-owner and philanthropist. Built in 1882, the building became one of Dr Barnardo's homes from 1945 to 1957. Further south, the magnificent Grand Hotel, built in 1872 stands perched above the cliffs on Percy Gardens, along with many other examples of fine buildings and houses, which form the structure of Tynemouth Village.

In 1856 Tynemouth consisted of little more than the area built up around Front Street.

BOROUGH OF TYNEMOUTH
COAT OF ARMS

A Coat of Arms was first proposed for the Borough of Tynemouth in October 1832. Although there are no known illustrations of the design, it was never officially adopted.

It was on 6th August 1849 that Tynemouth was granted a Charter of Incorporation and became a 'County Borough' which consolidated the neighbouring townships of Preston, Chirton, New York, North Shields and Cullercoats. As a result, a new Coat of Arms was designed.

This design has been in use since 1849 and is still evident in many places locally. It was commonly found on School Reports, Corporation Documents, Public Notices, Souvenir Trinkets and on the badges of various official employees to name but a few.

THE SHIELD at the centre of the Coat of Arms was that of the Prior of Tynemouth.

THE THREE CROWNS
These are actually depicted as coronets, and represent three ancient kings buried in the grounds of the priory; Oswin, 651 AD, Osred, 792 AD, Malcolm, 1093 AD.

Oswin
St Bede wrote of Oswin as tall, handsome, most courteous and generous to the poor, beloved of all men for his qualities of body and mind. Rather than have his soldiers butchered in battle he sent them home and gave himself up to his enemies, who murdered him. He was buried at Tynemouth. His tomb became a place of worship and many miracles were said to be performed there.

Osred
Northumbria was a place of violence and treachery. When Osred became king in 788 he was betrayed by his own nobles and became a monk at York. In 792 he attempted to regain his throne, but was betrayed again and put to death on the orders of King Ethelred. He was buried close to Osred at Tynemouth.

Malcolm
A fierce king of Scotland, Malcolm Canmore was forever raiding Northumbria. In 1093 his army met with William de Mowbray's forces near to Alnwick. In a fierce battle, 3,000 Scots were slain. A chapel was built on the spot where he died, but his body was brought to Tynemouth for burial.

THE SHIP
Sailing above the crest, is a ship in full sail which is indicative of the importance of both the River Tyne and the accompanying sea trade over the years.

THE PITMAN
Mining was first undertaken by the Monks of Tynemouth, and continued as an important trade in the area, so a pitman was chosen as a 'bearer' for the left side of the crest.

THE SEAMAN
Likewise, much of the local trade involved fishing and maritime activities, so a seaman was chosen as a bearer for the right side of the crest.

THE MOTTO

MESSIS AB ALTIS – this motto in Latin tells us why the pitman and the seaman were chosen as the bearers on the coat of arms of Tynemouth Borough. The literal translation in English means: 'Harvest from the Deep'.

The pitman worked deep below the surface, tunneling coal from the ground (Preston and Chirton Collieries).

The seaman or fisherman pulled fish from the depths of the sea. (Cullercoats and North Shields), hence the motto 'Harvest from the Deep'.

The County Borough of Tynemouth survived for 125 years before it ceased to exist when in 1974 it was absorbed within the new North Tyneside Council.

The historic Coat of Arms soon disappeared from use; however some elements of the design have since been adapted and incorporated within the present Coat of Arms for North Tyneside.

During the existence of the County Borough of Tynemouth, many examples and derivatives of the original Coat of Arms have appeared on schools, public buildings and parks in various formats.

In those days, this was perhaps seen as boasting a fine example of civic pride. For various reasons, many of these plaques and emblems have slowly disappeared and now, only a small handful remains.

The following list outlines those locations where, in 2014, the old Tynemouth Coat of Arms and its derivatives are still evident throughout the former borough:

1. Preston Avenue (Rear wall of King Edward Primary School).
2. Howard Street (Glass fanlight above door to old Borough Treasurer's office).
3. Oxford Street Railway Station (Mariners Point).
4. TVLB Watch House.
5. Tynemouth Park (Stone Planters).
6. Bath Arcade (Over door).
7. Tynemouth High School (Tynemouth College).

Above: The old Tynemouth Coat of Arms on Tynemouth High School (Tynemouth College).

Left: A stone planter in Tynemouth Park with the Coat of Arms in the centre.

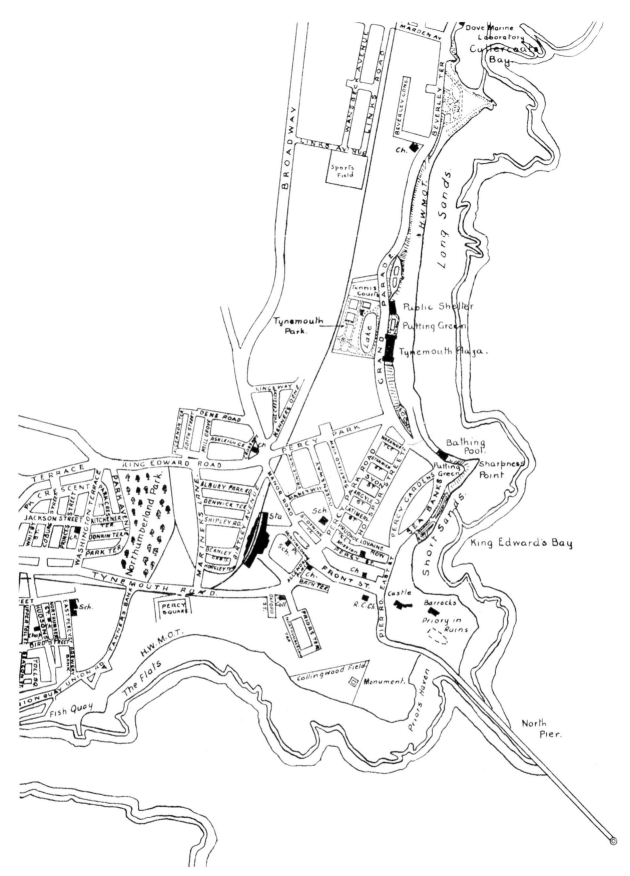

A map of Tynemouth taken from a 1932 Guide Book.

FOLKLORE

TYNEMOUTH FOLK SONG

The Cliffs of Old Tynemouth is a beautiful 'Shields' Folk Song, written in 1843 by David Ross Leitch. The song first appeared in a small pamphlet which formed the basis for a number of other 'Shields' songs which were later published in the *Shields Gazette* during the 1850s.

Oh! The Cliffs of Old Tynemouth they're wild and they're sweet,
And dear are the waters that roll at their feet;
And the old ruined Abbey, it ne'er shall depart;
Tis the star of my fancy, the home of my heart.

Oh! 'twas there that my childhood fled cheerful and gay,
There I loitered the morning of boyhood away,
And now as I wander the old beach alone,
The waves seem to whisper the names that are gone.

Twas there with my Alice I walked hand-in-hand,
While the wild waves in moonlight leapt o'er the bright sand;
And sweet were the echoes of the dark Cliffs above,
But oh! sweeter her voice as she murmured her love.

On thy waters, Old Tynemouth, throng seamen as brave
As e'er cheer'd in the battle, or conquer'd the wave;
And for sweet pretty maidens, seek England around,
Near the Cliffs of Old Tynemouth the fairest are found.

Other lands may be fairer, but nought can be seen,
Like the shore where our first love and boyhood have been;
Oh! give me the Cliffs and the wild roaring sea –
The Cliffs of old Tynemouth for ever for me.

The iconic landmarks of Tynemouth are depicted in this old painting.

THE GHOST OF TYNEMOUTH PRIORY

In the year 793, in an unprecedented attack which shocked the whole of Europe, a raiding party of Vikings from Norway attacked the North East coast of England concentrating their efforts towards Lindisfarne.

The monasteries that were exposed on the eastern coast of Northumbria were regarded as wealthy treasure houses that were an irresistible target for the Vikings.

Further attacks followed in 794 when the Vikings attacked the famous monastery at Jarrow, although on this occasion the Northumbrians were prepared for the attack and managed to surprise and utterly destroy the assailants, however further Viking raids on Lindisfarne and Jarrow continued throughout the year and by 800, monasteries at Whitby, Hartlepool and Tynemouth also became targets.

The ruins of Tynemouth Priory which are said to be haunted by the Ghost of Olaf the Viking.

The ruins of Tynemouth Priory and Castle are said to be haunted by the ghost of one of these Viking raiders who was badly wounded in a raid on Tynemouthshire during this time.

His name was Olaf, who was abandoned by the marauders and later nursed back to health by the Priory monks. It is said that Olaf was so grateful to the Monks for their help and care that he remained with them, eventually joining their community in the monastery.

In a subsequent Viking raid, some of the marauders returned, one of which happened to be Olaf's brother who was killed in the fierce fighting which ensued.

When he discovered the fate of his brother, Olaf was said to be so grief-stricken that he himself died whilst praying in the chapel soon afterwards.

When an east wind blows, it is said that Olaf's ghost can be seen wandering the castle grounds and looking wistfully out to sea, as he gazes back towards his Scandinavian homeland.

THE MONK'S STONE

Although no date seems apparent, the legend of the Monk's Stone gives a picture of monkish life in Tynemouth soon after the Norman Conquest. The tale has several variations, but the general interpretation is as follows:

A weary monk from Tynemouth Priory was travelling near to Seaton Delaval, and when passing a Mansion House (long before the construction of the present Delaval Hall), he smelled cooking, and wandered into the kitchen where a boar or hog was roasting.

The monk appealed to the cook to cut off the head of the roasting beast to quell his hunger, but was refused and told that the animal was being prepared for a banquet at the imminent return of the master – Lord Delaval who was temporarily out on a hunt.

The monk however waited until such time as the cook's back was turned, and immediately cut off its head and ran away with it, hoping to make good ground and arrive at Tynemouth Monastery before the theft was discovered by the master.

During the six mile journey, the Monk rested at Monkseaton for a while before continuing onwards.

Meanwhile, Lord Delaval came home from the hunt and was furious when he was informed about the loss of his titbit. He therefore mounted his horse, and galloped off at a high pace in search of the thieving monk.

As Lord Delaval approached Tynemouth, he came upon the monk, who was still in possession of the boar's head. Lord Delaval then chastised the monk by giving him a severe beating with his hunting whip. The

'O Horrid Dede, to Kill a Man for a Pigg's Hede'.

exhausted and injured monk was scarcely able to reach the monastery and had to be rescued by his fellow brethren.

The monk died within a year and a day, and Lord Delaval was charged with the murder, and by way of compromise, he was obliged to sign over various estates and lands to the monastery and set up an obelisk on the spot where he had chastised the monk.

The obelisk is a sandstone pillar, the remains of an ancient cross, at the base of which were carved the words: *'O Horrid Dede, to Kill a Man for a Pigg's Hede'*.

The exact location of the sandstone pillar is unconfirmed, but is described in historical publications as being in front of the 'Monks House', in a field at a farmstead not far from the road leading northward from Holy Saviors' Church. This would probably place the stone in the vicinity of the present day Monkstone Crescent, which took its name from this fanciful legend.

The original purpose of the pillar may have been to mark the limit of sanctuary assigned to the monastery of Tynemouth, however other theories suggest that it could have been a rood-stone or market-stone around which fairs were held in olden times. The stone has long since been removed, and has stood in the grounds of Tynemouth Priory since 1936.

JINGLING GEORDIE'S HOLE

The following article in the 1887 Monthly Chronicle suggests that fairies once lived in Tynemouth: *'Tynemouth, in the olden time (and that not so far back either) is declared to have been a favourite haunt of the fairies. An old woman, whom a friend of ours visited the other day to gather any particulars she might know respecting the mythical 'Jingler', was told that her recollections went back at least sixty years, and that the story was already an old one when she was a girl, but that she had herself actually seen the fairies, so that was no mere hearsay.'*

Inasmuch as the reference to the 'Jingler' is concerned, few people are aware of the existence of a mysterious cave situated in the cliff face on the promontory of Benebal Crag, next to King Edward's Bay just below Tynemouth Castle where infernal spirits are said to dwell.

Some sources suggest that many sinister creatures are dwelling in caves at Tynemouth and according to a poem in Hone's Table Book dated 1827; the inhabitants of these mysterious caves are infernal beasts and demons who are guarding a great wealth of treasure.

Of course many folklore legends have survived about these caves and 'Jingling Geordie's Hole' in particular. Although there are several variations of the tale, it was commonly held that the inhabitant of this cave was either a mysterious stranger who prowled about at nights making a clanking noise with chains and fetters or a wrecker with a jingling iron leg who lured ships to their destruction on the rocks below by exhibiting distraction lights at the cave entrance.

It has also been suggested that the 'Wytche of Tinemouth' lived there whilst others say it was a wizard, hence the cave sometimes being known as the 'Wizard's Cave'. This cave allegedly formed the entrance to a subterranean passage beneath the River Tyne by which the Monks of Tynemouth Priory are said to have visited their distant brethren in Jarrow. It was reputed to contain chambers, vaults and dungeons linking an outlying tower to the priory.

However, the legend best associated with 'Jingling Geordie's Hole' states that somewhere inside the cave, a fabulous amount of treasure was said to be concealed, and after a local young boy named Walter had this tale related to him by his mother, it became his lifelong ambition to find the truth and seek out the bounty.

Many years passed, and Walter grew up to attain a knighthood, after which he resolved to find the elusive treasure as part of his quest to become a valiant knight.

On the Eve of St John (24th June – once traditionally regarded as the day before Midsummer's Eve), Sir Walter armed himself, and ventured forth, making his way fearlessly into the depths of the cave, where he journeyed into a long dark passage before being met by spectres, fiends and dragons that attempted to distract and divert him. Sir Walter showed no fear and journeyed on before discovering a portal, in front of which a bugle hung from a golden cord, with which he blew three loud blasts causing the portal doorway to roll back. On opening, a vast chamber was revealed, the roof of which was supported by twelve pillars of Jasper and twelve of fine Crystal with twelve Gold lamps softly illuminating twelve altars of Onyx stone with burning incense. The floor sparkled with precious gems of Diamonds, Emeralds, Sapphires, Rubies, Amethyst, Topaz and Beryls which glittered in the soft light.

The treasures were removed by Sir Walter, who thereafter became a wealthy landowner and was later to become known as 'The Lord of a Hundred Castles'. The legend is mentioned in the following local folk song:

> *Down deep in the rock winds the pathway drear,*
> *And the yells of the spirits seem near and more near,*
> *And the flames from their eye-balls burn ghastly blue*
> *As they dance round the knight with a wild halloo.*
>
> *Fierce dragons with scales of bright burnished brass,*
> *Stand belching red fire where the warrior must pass;*
> *But rushes he on with his brand and his shield,*
> *And with loud shrieks of laughter they vanish and yield.*
>
> *Huge hell-dogs come baying with murd'rous notes,*
> *Sulphureous flames in their gaping throats;*
> *and they spring to, but shrinks not, brave Walter the Knight*
> *And again all is sunk in the darkness of night.*
>
> *It may not be sung what treasures were seen,*
> *Gold heaped upon gold, and emeralds green,*
> *And diamonds and rubies, and sapphires untold,*
> *Rewarded the courage of Walter the Bold.*

In 1874, the cave was destroyed in part by a fall of rock and the entrance has since been sealed up.

This may be for the good of everyone bearing in mind the infernal creatures which are reputed to live in there; however if you should be passing late at night and hear a distant jingling from the cliffs, perhaps it would be wise to increase your pace and hurry home!

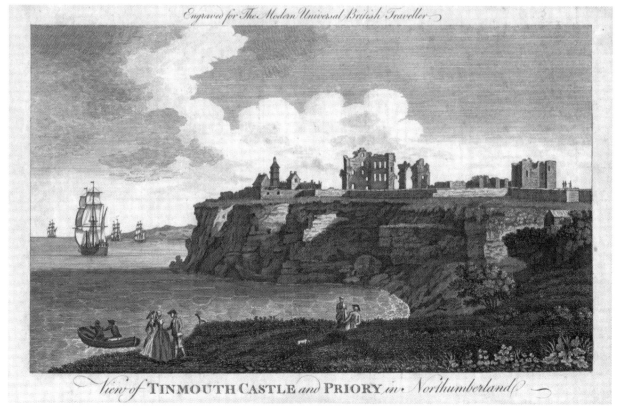

King Edward's Bay, Benebal Crag and Tynemouth Priory in 1790.

THE TALE OF WANDERING WILLIE

During the Spring of 1873, a shepherd was driving a flock of sheep from the Cheviot Hills in the far North of Northumberland intending to travel to the Cleveland hills assisted by his faithful Border Collie dog, 'Willie'.

After a journey of many miles, they arrived at the Old Steam ferry to cross the River Tyne at North Shields where they found everything completely different from the peace and tranquility of their native hillsides. Chimneys poured out smoke, there were rattles and bangs from the nearby shipyards, as well as the general noise, hustle and bustle of the nearby town.

Whilst waiting at the ferry landing, fear mounted in the sheep until such time they could stand it no longer, as a result of which they began to panic and scatter in all directions. Willie, the dog being good at his work ran after them as quick as a flash, but as the sheep had scattered so far in their panic, and it took him some time to round them up from some of the strange places they had used on their escape routes.

The dog eventually managed to round up the sheep, and direct the flock back to the shepherd waiting at the ferry, who made a quick count and discovered that there was at least one sheep missing. The shepherd then ordered Willie off, to go and look for it. Whilst the dog was making his search for the 'lost' sheep, the shepherd decided to have a quick re-count, and after making a thorough check, found that his first count was in fact wrong, and that all of the sheep were accounted for after having been safely returned in the first place.

Willie had still not returned when the ferry-boat arrived at the landing, so in order to save time, the shepherd herded all of the flock onto the boat. When the time came for the vessel to cast-off, there was still no sign of

North Shields Steam Ferry.

Willie, and so the ferry boat headed off across the Tyne to South Shields without him.

It was some hours later that Willie returned after having made a vain search only to find now, that his master and the flock had gone. Willie was probably confused, and then made his way off once more to look for the 'missing' sheep, but not being able to find it, returned once more to the ferry-landing, tired and hungry to look for his master, who was obviously nowhere to be seen.

People came and went on the ferry for the rest of the day, and Willie checked each and every one of them. Where could his master have gone?

Willie laid down in hope at the last place that he saw his master and waited. He was tired and hungry and now lost! Over the days that followed, Willie rummaged for food and drink, and spent countless hours on end waiting at the ferry-landing for his master to return.

He refused all offers of comfort, and even bared his teeth at anyone who ventured too close. He accepted only the food which was carefully placed within his reach, preferring to scavenge near to the waters edge for scraps and morsels. For over six months, the dog waited in the area for his master to return, and then one dark night, he decided to creep onto the ferry-boat in his relentless search. Willie was spotted by one of the crewmen, who caught hold of him and, unmercifully, threw him overboard. Willie knew that because he must find his master, he could not allow himself to die by drowning in the river, so despite strong undercurrents in the water, he only just managed to swim ashore – cold, wet and shivering.

Over the months that followed, Willie evolved a system where he would make checks on the ferry-boat to see if the cruel crewman who threw him overboard was there. If he was, then Willie would stay ashore, but if he was not on the boat – he would make numerous journeys to and fro across the river in his relentless and unending search.

By the Autumn of that year, Willie's master had returned to the area, after his long and arduous journey, and learned of the dogs long and lonely wait, but because of the shepherd's haste to return to the Northumbrian Hills, they sadly missed their re-union by only a matter of minutes at the ferry landings.

Many more months passed and Willie, not realising that his master had now passed by on his return north, succumbed to the goodwill and hospitality of friendly passers-by.

Willie became well known to many of the locals, who would occasionally manage to encourage him to their homes and feed him but, irrespective of that, the outcome was always the same. Willie would stay with his new-found friend for anywhere between a day and a couple of weeks before running off to return to the ferry-landing to continue the search for his master.

As the year progressed into the winter, concern was beginning to grow in relation to Willie's health, as well as grave doubts about whether or not he would be able to survive the winter weather.

Willie was by now growing very thin, frail, bedraggled and dirty, but had managed to become more trusting and responded well to the kindness of his regular friends.

Over the months that followed, a Mr Thomas Hudson of North Shields became one of Willie's best friends and who, on realising that the dog was close to death, took him to his home, where he was cleaned up, fed regularly and nursed back to health.

A Mr Frazer, from South Shields, who was an expert metalworker and a long time friend of Thomas Hudson, made a fine brass collar for Willie, which the dog seemed well proud of, but unfortunately it did not last long, as it was soon stolen from the dog's neck. The despicable theft angered many local people.

Willie regularly made off to his place near the ferry-landing in the hope of meeting up with his now long gone master.

The painstaking result of his search, had taught the dog his way around North and South Shields, and passengers would arrive at the ferry-landing perhaps asking directions to the railway station, only to be told – 'Just follow Wandering Willie.'

North Shields Ferry Landing.

North Shields Railway Station in 1873.

The dog would lead people to the station gates, and then return quickly back to the ferry-landing and perform a similar task on the other side of the river.

Willie became well known and made hundreds of friends amongst the ferry passengers, crews and workmen on both sides of the river.

On Sundays, Willie would always make his way to Tynemouth where he would wander round for several hours before returning as usual to the ferry-landing in the unending search for his lost master.

As the years passed by, and Willie grew older, he became tired and weary, so one of the ferry crewmen, Mr Ralph Cruikshanks, decided that it would be right to take Willie home with him to Dean Street in South Shields, where the now aged dog could live the rest of his life in the comfort of a home, with all the food, kindness and sleep as Willie could manage.

Mr Cruikshanks was asked on many occasions to part with the dog, and even refused to accept the sum of £50 when offered! They became the best of friends until sadly, in April 1882 Willie died of old age.

Mr Cruikshanks had became so attached to Willie, that he decided to give the carcass to a Mr G. Green, a well-known Taxidermist in South Shields, who made such an excellent job on Willie that he now stands preserved forever, on display for all to see in what has been his home for many years now – behind a glass case in the hallway of the Turks Head Pub, on Front Street, Tynemouth.

Wandering Willie

THE COAST AND RIVER
THE LONG SANDS

Tynemouth Long Sands stretch for over half a mile from the village of Cullercoats at the northern end to the rocky outcrop known as Sharpness Point which guards King Edward's Bay at the southern end. Partially backed by shallow cliffs and sand dunes, this illustrates the characteristics of a rural beach in an urban location.

At low tide several patches of rocks are accessible on the sands themselves and together with the larger outcrop at Cullercoats known as Saddle Rocks; these provide endless rock pools in which to catch crabs or spot sea anemones. These rocks join Tynemouth North Point, at the head of the Long Sands, the most easterly of which is called Crab Hill and is visible at low tide.

A few hundred yards south, a small rocky outcrop known as Bears Head Rock sits adjacent to the Long Sands, almost opposite the site of the former Beaconsfield House. In the late 18th century, sea-bathing became fashionable in Tynemouth and the beach became a popular venue during the summer months.

The Long Sands is popular all year round, though especially in the summer season and over recent years, the sea towards the southern part of the beach has become increasingly fashionable with surfers.

King Edward's Bay to the south of Sharpness Point, is a small sandy cove approximately 200 metres long enclosed by cliffs and steep grass banks, and dominated by the ruins of Tynemouth Castle and Priory on the headland above, which is known as Benebal Crag. Beyond this headland, a small beach known locally as Priors Haven is situated within the mouth of the Tyne. It is a small cove which is sheltered between the Priory and the Spanish Battery, and was extremely popular with Victorian bathers and is now home to the local rowing and sailing clubs.

The following is a very colourful description of Tynemouth Long Sands, taken word for word from an old guidebook dated 1912: *'The Long Sands are seen to advantage from the Palace Terrace, and the descent thereto is easy. They form an admirable playground, being broad and smooth, and extending in a graceful curve for a considerable length. Their central portion is the best for bathing purposes, and here the bathing machines are numerous.*

Tynemouth Palace and Long Sands in 1912, showing the Bathing Machines and Rowing Boats described.

A short distance to the right of the Palace a large number of rowing boats are drawn up on the beach. Near the foot of the road down to the beach at the west end of the sands is a spa well or spring, the water of which has certain medicinal properties. Adjoining the Long Sands is King Edward's Bay, a charming little sheltered cove, which is exceedingly popular. An afternoon spent on the Sands watching the youngsters at play with bucket and spade, or studying the various characteristics of the good-natured crowd, need be by no means dull, while the rocks and pools are a constant source of attraction to many visitors, old and young. Northumbrians never wait to be amused, but are ever enterprising in finding means for beguiling the hours spent on the margin of the sea'.

One of the earliest known photographs of Tynemouth, is this view of the Long Sands which is believed to date to 1860, long before Tynemouth Palace, St George's Church and Beaconsfield House were built.

Tynemouth Beach, from a similar viewpoint. The sands are almost packed to capacity on a summer's day in 1946.

TYNEMOUTH OUTDOOR SWIMMING POOL

Tynemouth outdoor swimming pool was first opened on 30th May 1925. It was automatically filled by the incoming tide and was for many years a popular venue for families and holidaymakers.

This was a 'Boom' time for seaside lidos and open air pools where some of the hardier folk thought nothing of taking a plunge in the chilly waters. During the 1930s a total of 180 lidos and pools were built throughout the UK to add to the 50 which had already been constructed in the previous decade and they soon became a symbol of civic pride and progress.

Tynemouth Swimming Pool in its 1930s Heyday.

Many Swimming galas and competitions were held at Tynemouth Pool over the years, however after much neglect by the local authority, the pool fell into disuse and became derelict. Perhaps the advent of cheap foreign travel was partly to blame, but a 1960 report suggested that swimming pools should be housed indoors with buildings that were capable of catering for a range of sports, and so the 'Leisure Centre' was born.

In 1996 the council made an effort to revamp Tynemouth Pool under the guise of converting it to a 'Rock Pool' by scattering

1948 – Still in its Heyday.

large stones and boulders throughout. This was a disastrous failure and as the neglect continued, what was once a fine outdoor lido soon became a controversial eyesore.

60 years later – A derelict eyesore.

A proposal to concrete over the site and convert it into a possible venue for cultural and sporting activities was met with hostile objections by many local residents who wanted to see the pool turned back into a swimming facility. As a result, a local group was formed under the name 'Friends of Tynemouth Outdoor Pool', who are currently working with North Tyneside Council on viable plans for the future development of the pool.

THE LION'S HEAD FOUNTAIN

An old mineral spring which fed the Engine Well during the early 1820s helped to establish Tynemouth as a Spa resort as it was widely believed that the water in this area had health-giving properties. In 1862, the popularity of this belief resulted in the erection of a large fountain on Tynemouth Long Sands near Grand Parade at the bottom of Percy Park. This ornate fountain, which was approximately 10 feet in height was constructed to cover the Engine Well and became known as the 'Lion's Head Fountain' because water from the spring flowed through an ornamental lion's head.

The fountain was set against a retaining wall, backing onto the dunes with a cobbled pathway leading towards the sea. It was in regular use until the 1950s when it ran into a decline and was gradually reclaimed and buried by tons of sand which blew over it in the following years.

This 1910 image of Tynemouth Long Sands shows the Lion's Head Fountain towards the lower right corner of the picture.

This occurred at a time when hygiene regulations decreed that the water purity had to be checked on a daily basis to ensure that no contaminants had entered the flow, however the spring water eventually became seriously polluted by effluent from flooded mine workings and was totally unfit for human consumption, so it was diverted away from the fountain.

The water was redirected to a brick sump which faced the lion, and then through an outflow pipe to a steel one-way shutter valve situated approximately 100 yards down the beach to flow into the sea. This valve gradually disintegrated allowing incoming tides to slowly push sand up the pipe. The long term result of this was that the pipe became blocked right up to the brick sump. By 1992, the subsequent build up of pressure from the head forced the water out of the inspection hatch which caused flooding to the nearby cafe situated at the bottom of the adjacent ramp. Contractors were called in to trace the pipe and the blockage was eventually cleared. During this operation, part of the structure was unearthed by a JCB when

The Lion's Head Fountain, c. 1900.

it accidentally hit the fountain, breaking off part of the sandstone bowl. This was not repaired but, instead, placed into temporary storage.

In the meantime, the late Mr Will Hogg, a resident of Tynemouth who had served with the Tynemouth Volunteer Life Brigade (TVLB) for almost 25 years became an active campaigner to have the fountain excavated and restored, however the finances required were unavailable. On 23rd October 2010, a charity event was organised to raise funds for the TVLB by uncovering the 10 foot high fountain as a tribute to Will who died tragically in September 2009 during a charity swimming event which took place close by. The event was designed to allow members of the public to catch a glimpse of this beautiful Victorian Masterpiece as 600 tonnes of sand were removed to expose the full beauty of the structure which for a short time was on view for all to see.

North Tyneside Council ordered that the fountain be reunited with its missing sandstone bowl, and reburied beneath the sand soon afterwards in order to protect and preserve the fountain safely until such time as finances are available to allow for restoration work to be carried out. This event raised over £3,000 which in modern times is the largest single amount ever raised for

The Lion's Head Fountain – uncovered in October 2010.

the TVLB. Although not a listed building or structure, the fountain is recorded with North Tyneside Council on the local list as being an item of special architectural interest.

Will Hogg, was a well known and highly respected resident of the area. He was born on 1st January 1950 at Dilston, Northumberland and had lived in Tynemouth for over 30 years where he served locally as a beach and pool lifeguard from 1967 to 1971.

His father, Jack Hogg was the Foreshore Officer at Tynemouth from 1967 to 1981 and part of his duties involved making sure that the Lion's Head Fountain was dug out each summer by the lifeguards. Although it was not buried as deep in the sand as it is now, it was still maintained through the summer months and this is undoubtedly where Will's fascination with the fountain originated.

Will was also a swimming teacher and leisure manager at Tynemouth and Whitley Bay Swimming Pools from 2000 to 2009 and he joined the Tynemouth Volunteer Life Brigade (TVLB) on 12th March 1984 and served with them for over 25 years. In 1994, Will was elected as Captain of the Brigade and in 2006 he became Chairman.

During his service with the TVLB, he had taken part in more than 500 sea rescues. In 2007, TVLB was awarded Her Majesty the Queen's Award for Voluntary Service which Will received and accepted on behalf of the Brigade from the Lord Lieutenant of Tyne and Wear.

THE 1913 LANDSLIP

During November 1913, a massive landslip occurred at Tynemouth when over 80 yards of the cliff face below Sea Banks (the road running in a curve opposite Percy Gardens) collapsed. As a result, a large section of the roadway became unsafe and impassable, and the private thoroughfare at the south entrance to Percy Gardens was closed to all traffic, as there were indications of further ground movement. Falls of earth continued

for some days and a further section of roadway next to the lodge cottage and southern gate entrance of Percy Gardens was rendered unstable. Investigations later attributed the cause to a constant trickle of water from an old well, which existed prior to the road being built.

Sea Banks, 2010.

The constant flow over the years appears to have weakened a seam lying above a layer of shale, causing the overlying rock to collapse. The roadway had to be closed for some time, whilst stabilisation and major repair work was carried out.

In 1915, a series of stone arches were constructed in order to support the new road above. The arches were set into the existing cliff face for strength and stability, and are still visible from King Edward's Bay. In more recent years, the open arches were completely sealed up for structural and safety reasons.

TYNEMOUTH LIGHTHOUSE

There has been a lighthouse at Tynemouth for well over 800 years, and the first indication of this was in the 12th century, when monks had kept a light burning in a church tower on the headland at Tynemouth Priory.

In 1664, at the order of Colonel Villiers (Governor of Tynemouth Castle) the light was replaced with a lighthouse which was erected on the north east corner of the headland at Benebal Crag. It was built of stone probably taken from the ruined Priory and stood over 79 feet high with a roofed top and was enclosed on three sides.

The keeper lived in the base with his family and it his job to keep the coal fire at the top of the tower burning brightly on the incoming tide in all weathers. It was partly rebuilt in 1775, and in 1802 the coal light was replaced by a revolving oil lamp with reflectors.

By the 1890s, visibility problems arose with the old lighthouse which burned and emitted an orange-red light which was often obscured by smoke from the steam ships and the local industry which was then building up on the River Tyne.

Trinity House (which dates back to 1514) therefore decided that the lighthouse should be brought up to date, but were opposed by the military authorities, who wanted to claim the site for emplacement of a large gun, which they claimed to be necessary for coastal defence.

Trinity House was forced to agree to the proposal and, as a result, St Mary's (Bates) Island at Whitley Bay was chosen as the most convenient site to replace the old lighthouse.

When St Mary's Lighthouse eventually came into service in 1898, the structure on the headland at Benebal Crag was demolished.

The present lighthouse on Tynemouth North Pier was commissioned by the Port of Tyne Authority as a separate entity, but was never intended as a replacement for the original headland beacon.

This 1800s engraving looks south across the River Tyne to Benebal Crag headland, where the extent of Tynemouth Priory and Castle become apparent. The old lighthouse which acted as a guide to shipping entering the River Tyne is visible on the headland.

TYNEMOUTH NORTH PIER

Prior to the construction of the North and South Piers at the mouth of the Tyne, many ships were wrecked and it was impossible for shipping to leave the river when an easterly gale blew. In 1850, the Tyne Improvement Commission was formed to take control of the river, and incorporate the responsibility of creating a safe harbour of refuge at the mouth of the Tyne.

In 1852, an Act of Parliament was passed authorising a massive engineering project which would eventually see the construction of two stone piers and lighthouses. Although always referred to as such, these are not piers at all – they are actually called 'Breakwaters'. (A pier is defined as a platform extending from a shore over water and supported by piles or pillars and a breakwater is defined as a structure which protects a harbour or shore from the full impact of the waves.) Despite this terminology, nine eminent engineers of the day submitted designs for both the North and South 'Piers' with the accepted design being submitted by Mr James Walker, president of the Institution of Civil Engineers (1835-45).

On 15th June 1854, foundation stones were laid and work commenced on the North Pier, which was originally designed as a curve, and intended to be a mirror image of the South Pier (construction of which started two years later in 1856). It was estimated that the North Pier would be completed within a seven year time span; however the project was plagued by disasters. The task was enormous, and it soon became obvious that the work would extend well beyond the anticipated completion date. By December 1867, only 1,920 feet of the pier had been constructed, before severe gales, combined with the fury of the North Sea breached and destroyed almost 480 feet of the stone structure. It was later established that the foundations had not been sunk deep enough to withstand the powerful force of the North Sea. Repair work was effected, and by 1893 the pier was almost complete, but movement of the structure was detected during the severe winter storms of that year.

Breached stonework on the North Pier in January 1897.

In 1894, attempts were made to repair the damaged blocks of stone, but in 1895 further movement was detected, and several more stone blocks had suffered significant damage. By this time, the curved pier was complete and measured 2,959 feet in length, including the lighthouse.

During freak gales and heavy seas lasting 48 hours in January 1897, the North Pier was once again breached, resulting in extensive damage. 110 feet of stonework collapsed, leaving the lighthouse 'marooned'. The breach grew, until it was almost 100 yards wide.

In 1898, it was decided that the pier would have to be completely rebuilt, with the contract being awarded to the firm of Sir John Jackson. The pier was redesigned from that of a curved structure, to a straight line, and in October of that year, rebuilding work commenced. The old sections of pier were used as shelter when work on the new section began. Most of the work went according to plan, and by 15th January 1908, the North lighthouse was commissioned.

In 1909, the new pier was complete, and eventually opened on 1st April – not within seven years as first planned, but a staggering 55 years after work had first begun. The construction work has been recorded as one of the most difficult undertakings of its kind ever carried out in this country, and is regarded as a wonderful monument of skill and dogged determination.

The pier has stood solidly since its completion, and has continued to withstand the fury of the North Sea. The original cost of the North Pier was £568,000; however the reconstruction work added an extra £450,000 taking the total build costs up to £1,018,000. Over three million tons of stonework was used to construct both the North and South piers. The North Pier measures 899 metres in length and the lighthouse is 26 metres in height with a white navigation light over-arcing the horizon for a distance of 26 miles. The distance between the round heads of the two piers is 360 metres.

The Port of Tyne Authority conduct regular safety inspections of the North Pier to ensure the continual safety of the structure.

The pier has a broad walkway on top, and on the leeward side there is evidence of a former lower-level railway track used by

The curvature of the original North Pier is evident in this 1895 image.

trains and cranes for maintenance work and the loading of ships. This railway track was once connected to and serviced from the nearby Oxford Street Goods Station.

A little known fact about Tynemouth Pier is that a hard porcelain or glazed stoneware Doll is set into the stonework of the pier wall. The reason for this has never been confirmed with any certainty; however various theories have been put forward over the years.

It is highly likely though, that the doll was embedded into the wet concrete of the lighthouse wall, by one of the workers involved in the construction project. A similar doll is also embedded in the wall of the South Pier at its half-way point. The ravages of more than a hundred years of stormy seas and erosion have completely worn away these dolls beyond recognition and over the years, thousands of fingers have touched, rubbed, scratched, and picked at them, leaving little more than a basic impression.

A plaque situated at the commencement of the North Pier commemorates its completion.

Construction work progresses on rebuilding the new North Pier, c. 1899.

THE BLACK MIDDENS

For centuries the mouth of the Tyne was a place of shifting sandbanks and dangerous rocks. Most feared of all were the notorious Black Midden rocks. According to local folklore, these rocks were thrown there by the devil in an attempt to curb the wealthy sea trade of Newcastle (which was never achieved). Usually covered at high tide, the Black Middens have been responsible for many shipwrecks and over the years, have caused the death by drowning of hundreds of mariners and their passengers. Most poignantly, they all died within a few yards of the safety of the shore. During three days of blizzards and storms in 1864, the Black Middens claimed four ships and thirty four lives.

These dangerous rocks, which are now overlooked by Admiral Lord Collingwood's monument, were instrumental in bringing about the formation of the first ever Volunteer Life Brigade service which was

The Black Middens in 1912.

established at Tynemouth in 1864. The register shown at the end of this section lists those vessels which have run aground on these rocks, however the list is by no means comprehensive as many other ships have been similarly stranded or wrecked on the nearby Spanish Battery Rocks which form part of the same outcrop.

Before the North and South Piers were built, the sea would roar in from the south and thunder against the cliffs which made the river entrance an extremely hostile and treacherous area. In the early days, these black rocks formed sand bars which stretched across the river and moved with every tide. With one tide there could be up to seventeen foot of water, and with the next tide it might only be six foot of water making navigation on the river extremely difficult and dangerous, however after construction work on the piers had been completed, the river became easier to dredge, thereby enabling a safer shipping flow into the harbour.

The term 'Midden' is generally a local term, and the strict dictionary definition is: *'An accumulation of refuse, especially from a prehistoric kitchen fire; a dunghill or manure heap.'*

Whichever way these hazardous rocks may be defined, the infamous Black Middens have existed for centuries and remain a sinister reminder of darker days.

On the 8th December 1899, the cargo ship SS Craigneuk was entering the River Tyne when she struck the end of the North Pier. The vessel drifted onto the nearby Battery Rock beside the Black Middens. The Tynemouth Volunteer Life Brigade put a line on board and ten crewmen one woman and a child were landed by Breeches Buoy.

A guide to Shipwrecks and Groundings recorded on the Black Middens since 1810:

Year	Vessel Name	Vessel Type	Year	Vessel Name	Vessel Type
1811	CADIZ PACKET	Brig	1864	AMY ROBSART	Square Rigged
	TELEMACHUS	Brig		JOHN SLATER	Fishing Vessel
1815	MERCURY	Brig		STANLEY	Steamship
1818	JANE	Collier		ARDWELL	Schooner
1821	CHARLES	Brig	1865	EARL PERCY	Steamship
	THOMAS	Brig		RINGWOOD	Brig
1827	BETSY CAIRNS	Collier		UNION	Barque
1829	ECONOMY	Brig		BORDER CHIEFTAIN	Brig
1830	GLATTON	Sloop	1870	ANNE	Brig
1831	FANNY	Brig		HELENA	Barque
	LIBERTY	Brig		LIGHT OF HARLEM	Schooner
	VICTORY	Brig		SUSANNAH	Brigantine
1838	SPRIGHTLY	Square Rigged	1871	CYNTHIA ANNE	Brig
	TRIO	Square Rigged		ADMIRAL CODRINGTON	Schooner
1841	ALLENDALE	Brig		JABEZ	Brig
1842	PERCY	Brig		ORONICO	–
1843	EMILY	Fore/Aft Rigged		BRITISH QUEEN	–
	PERCY	Square Rigged	1874	BREEZE	Steamship
1845	MARIA	Dutch Galliot	1876	SEVEN SONS	Schooner
1846	BRITAIN	Sailing Vessel	1879	MARY	Steamship
1847	JAMES	Brig	1880	JCHANVA	–
	LADY ANNE	Brig	1881	FAITHFUL	Square Rigged
1848	GEORGE	Brig		IRON CROWN	Fore/Aft
1850	EDWARD	Sailing Vessel			Rigged
	LUNA	Fishing Vessel	1882	FINLAY	Steamer
	MARRY ANNE	Square Rigged		PROVIDENCE	Steamer
1852	JOHN WESLEY	–		RHINELAND	Barque
1853	SYLPH	Sloop		R.W. BOYD	Steamer
1854	LIVELY	Schooner	1883	AN YEAN	Steamship
	KATE	Schooner		CACTUS	Brig
	NAPOLEON	Schooner		JANET IZAT	Square Rigged
	EURAYTHA	–		PERTH	Lugger
	ARETHUSA	–		ALEAS	Schooner
	ANNE	–	1885	SIR ROBERT PEEL	Barque
	ANTELOPE	–	1891	PEGGY	Schooner
	ELIZABETH	–	1895	RUPERT	Brigantine
	NEW MESSENGER	–	1899	MALTBY	Cargo Ship
1855	AMULET	Square Rigged	1900	ANNA EUGEN	Steamship
	REDWING	Fore/Aft Rigged	1908	NORFOLK	Steamer
1857	LA VIGIE	Square Rigged	1912	CAPE COLONNA	Steamer
1859	ELIZABETH	Fishing Vessel	1914	KENNILWORTH	Steamship
	SIR WILLIAM CURTIS	Square Rigged	1916	BESSHEIM	Steamship
1860	HUGH	Fishing Vessel	1933	EILANDE	Steamship
1861	MARINER	Cargo Ship	1951	HMS BRAVE	Drillship
1862	NAUTILUS	Square Rigged	1957	POLAR PRINCE	Fishing Vessel
	MARY CAMPBELL	Brig	1974	OREGIS	Oil Rig
1863	TELEGRAPH	Brig			Support Ship
				NORTHSIDER	Tug

The list above is not exhaustive or comprehensive and gives only a general selection of vessels recorded as victims claimed directly by the Black Middens Rocks. The nearby Spanish Battery, Castle Rocks and Herd Sands have also been responsible for many other similar shipwrecks not recorded here.

STREETS & PLACES
EAST STREET

East Street is a very short section of road which runs from the foot of Tynemouth Front Street and connects with Sea Banks at Percy Gardens (ending at the junction with Lovaine Row). Perhaps one of the earliest photographs of East Street is dated c. 1870

(*right*), and depicts Ralph Pigg's grocery shop and Post Office which stood on a site close to the present Gibraltar Rock Public House. During the 1800s and early 1900s, East Street was just a narrow road which was crowded with popular Cafe's, Tea & Cocoa Rooms. Some of these establishments were simply temporary wooden structures which had been constructed on the cliffside of King Edward's Bay and were precariously balanced against the bankside cliffs by wooden props and support posts.

Towards the 1920s, most of these structures were removed as they were deemed unsafe. Following this, East Street was widened and the cliff tops were rehabilitated.

Several buildings on the clifftops at East Street overlooked King Edward's Bay and were evident at Tynemouth from the late 1800s to the early 1900s before their removal and demolition for safety reasons.

Much of East Street was once taken up by various refreshment houses, which extended along the street as far as Sea Banks. An extract from the 1912 Wards Directory indicates the following establishments were trading here;

1 East Street	J. Stephenson (Gibraltar Rock Inn)
3 East Street	W. Ferguson (Refreshment Rooms)
5 East Street	Mrs I. Gilmore (Priory Inn)
9 East Street	J. Heron (Refreshment Rooms)
Sea Banks	Miss C. Brown (Refreshment Rooms)
Sea Banks	A. Clements (Refreshment Rooms)
Sea Banks	W.M. Bell (Refreshment Rooms)

LIGHTBOWN'S HOTEL

Lightbown's Temperance Hotel & Restaurant was situated on the corner of East Street and Percy Street. (Collectively, the address was Nos 85 & 86 Percy Street and also No 8 East Street, Tynemouth).

The following colourful description is an extract from an 1890s guidebook:

'Lightbown's Temperance Hotel & Restaurant is probably the best known establishment of its kind in Tynemouth and neighbourhood. Mr Lightbown has long been recognised as a caterer of the highest grade of excellence, the large and continuous business which he conducts with so much success and satisfaction to his patrons being in evidence on this point. The premises are admirably situated about five minutes from the railway station and four minutes from the Tynemouth Palace, the pier being close at hand. The hotel has fourteen comfortable bedrooms, besides sitting rooms, while the restaurant has six spacious rooms devoted to purposes of public refreshment. The rooms are substantially furnished and convenient in every way, accommodating parties for dinners, luncheons, teas etc. while an excellent sea view is enjoyed. The special feature of the restaurant business is the provision of abundant food of the best kind at the lowest possible prices. Home-made confectionery is provided. Pies are a speciality, fresh daily.'

FRONT STREET

The present course of Front Street was once the main access route leading to Tynemouth Castle and Priory. It always has been, and perhaps still is, the most significant street in Tynemouth forming the core of the village, which over a number of years has been built up to provide some architecturally stunning buildings, many of them Grade II listed and all with a fascinating history behind them.

Front Street, as seen from Tynemouth Castle in 1905.

The wide street was first divided in the 1940s with the siting of car parking facilities throughout its central length and, today, this has developed further with the construction of some kerbstones and pedestrian refuges. Over the years, however, many other significant changes have occurred as many of the old established shops and businesses have gradually disappeared. Today, Front Street could perhaps be best regarded as the main focal point in the village, where many of the old buildings now accommodate a wide selection of shops, pubs, restaurants and cafés to form the heart of the village.

This early 1860 image of Tynemouth Front Street looks west towards Holy Saviours Church (visible in the distance). Front Street at this time was a continuous road, linking with Manor Terrace (now Manor Road) and connecting the road from Holy Saviours to Tynemouth Castle and Priory. There was no break in the street until the late 1800s when the smaller of the two buildings in the photograph were demolished to make way for the development of Percy Park Road.

A similar view of the same area, dated 1902, shows many of the same buildings standing with the exception of those cleared in order to lay out Percy Park Road, which incorporated the construction of a new two storey building situated on the corner of the street.

Front Street, looking west from the Arcade, c. 1904. The original Percy Arms is visible to the right of the picture with an awning outside.

JACKSON'S BILLIARD ROOMS

The Arcade, Tynemouth

English Billiards dates its origin to the early 1800s and its popularity increased as an indoor sport throughout the Victorian and Edwardian eras. Jackson's Private and Public Billiard Rooms were situated above the Arcade on Tynemouth Front Street, and were first established in 1859. An account taken from a late 1800s guide book describes them as follows: *'These admirable billiard rooms are situated in the Front Street adjoining the Bath Hotel, entering by the first door in the Arcade. The fittings and general*

furnishings of the interior are in good taste, particular attention being paid to the ventilation, while the tables are of the first quality, by Burroughs and Watts and are in excellent playing condition. These rooms are well known to a large circle of patrons, who find them admirably adapted for purposes of social enjoyment, as well as indulging in the fascinating game. Refreshments of all kinds can be had on the shortest notice. The position as noted is most central and convenient, especially for guests at the hotels and boarding houses, a private room being reserved for lady players. The basement property is occupied by a branch bank, and large chemist and druggist's shop. The rooms are an essential benefit to this seaside resort, and we have therefore, pleasure in noticing them in a work like this.'

BROWN'S (Fishmongers)

32 & 33 Front Street, Tynemouth
Mr W.B. Brown was a Fishmonger, Poulterer and Ice Merchant with his shop being situated at Nos 32 & 33 Front Street. An advertisement in an early 1900s guidebook describe the business and premises as follows:
'The shop is admirably situated in the main business thoroughfare of the town, and is one of the best equipped premises of the kind in the North of England. There is a handsome double frontage and the interior arrangements are excellent. No expense has been spared in the fitting and decorating of these premises, Carrara marble having been lavishly used for slabs, counters and fittings. The floor is composed of a neat inlay of Spanish and Carrara marble combined; there is also a lavish display of mirrors, which materially adds to the brightness of the establishment. Attached to these premises is a neatly fitted dining-room, where fish dinners and teas can always be obtained. Visitors to Tynemouth would do well to give the establishment a call.'
The building still survives and for many years has been better known to the locals as Marshall's Fish & Chip Shop.

J.F. FISCHER (Pork Butcher)

42 Front Street, Tynemouth
Standing at the door of the shop, Mr John Frederick Fischer was a wholesale and retail pork butcher who also specialised in the preparation of table delicacies such as cooked meat, sausages and celebrated pork pies, all of which were manufactured on the premises. Hot pork sandwiches were also sold from the shop. Situated at No 42 Front Street, directly next door to the present Turks Head Pub, the building was

demolished in later years to make way for the modern development at the foot of Front Street.

THE TREVELYAN HOTEL

70 Front Street, Tynemouth

Situated immediately next to Messrs. J. Young's drapery store, the full title of this inconspicuous building was the Trevelyan Temperance Hotel and Boarding House which stood at No 70 Front Street. The entrance door is to the right of the picture and a sign above it advertises dinners and teas. Little is known of the hotel, however, during the early 1900s the proprietress was recorded as a Mrs White. An early brochure colourfully describes the premises and accommodation in the language of the day as follows: *'There are the usual dining and sitting-rooms, which are solidly and well-furnished, with eight admirable and well-aired bedrooms with sanitary arrangements of the most approved kind. The food, cooking etc. are of the best, and the charges moderate, the most perfect cleanliness being noticeable in all departments. Mrs White makes it a point to supervise the details of the establishment and see that the wants of guests are supplied in every way and a large and well-established connection is enjoyed.'* S. Greenwell's drapery shop was situated on the ground floor.

ALLARDS (Grocers)

75 Front Street, Tynemouth

Mr. S.L. Allard was a Grocer and Provision Dealer who ran shops at No 75 Front Street, Tynemouth and also at No 186 Whitley Road, Whitley Bay. Allard's were particularly well known in the area and this double-fronted store adjoined the Congregational Church (Land of Green Ginger). The shop contained five departments which embraced teas, coffees, cocoas & chocolates, general groceries, dessert fruits, confectionery, provisions, drugs, homeopathic medicines and aerated waters. Several changes have taken place over the years and from the early 1970s to 2011, the premises became a motor factors trading as 'Auto Silencers'.

POLETTI'S BAZAAR

43 & 44 Front Street, Tynemouth

One of the best known institutions in Tynemouth was Poletti's Bazaar, situated at Nos 43 and 44 Front Street. The shop was first established in 1859 by the late Mr. C. Poletti, which, on his death in 1878, came into the hands of his brother-in-law, Mr Thomas Baker. Situated on Front Street close to the junction with East Street, just a few yards away from the Clock Tower, this colourful shop had a handsome double frontage and was always well-stocked with a huge variety of assorted items which included French and German fancy goods, jewellery, china and glass ornaments, all kinds of toys, opera and field glasses, dressing cases and workboxes, cabinet goods, clocks, silver chains, biscuit boxes, leather goods, eye glasses, brushes, combs, picture frames,

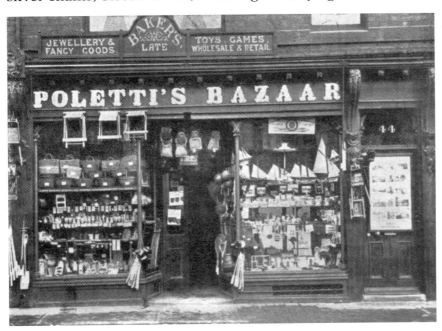

along with postcards and pictures showing local and general views of the area. All the novelties of the season were stocked, and the proprietor was an agent for the best makers of cricket, football and lawn tennis goods. A special department inside the shop catered for the repair of jewellery. The shop adjoined J.F. Fischer's Pork Butchers shop (also covered in this section) and similarly was lost to modern development.

MESSRS J. YOUNG & Co (Drapers)

71 & 72 Front Street, Tynemouth

One of the larger stores that were situated on Tynemouth Front Street was that of Messrs. J. Young and Co, Drapers, Dressmakers and Silk Mercers. Occupying premises

situated at Nos 71 & 72 Front Street on the south side of the road, close to the Congregational Church, the premises originally had an extensive double-frontage, with attractive window displays which included gloves, corsets, blouses, ribbons, flowers, feathers and hats. Inside, there were special showrooms for millinery and dressmaking, with several fitting and workrooms available. The premises were altered and, in recent years, became the Co-op.

T. YOUNG (Gentlemen's Outfitter)

15 Front Street, Tynemouth

Mr Thomas Young was a Hosier and Men's Mercer who ran his shop at No 15 Front Street, on the site of what is now Tynemouth Social Club. Mr Young also sold cycling accessories and was an agent for 'Rover' and 'Meteor' Cycles which accounts for the unusual presence of a Bicycle displayed in the shop window.

R. CHAMPNEY (Butcher)

23 Front Street, Tynemouth

Mr R. Champney was a master butcher who first established his business in Middle Street, Tynemouth in 1862. Increasing trade necessitated a move to larger premises at No 23 Front Street in the late 1800s and the following description of the business was taken from an early 1900s Tynemouth guidebook: *'Champney's is one of the oldest as well as best-known establishments of its class in Tynemouth. Mr. Champney, the proprietor started the business in Middle Street, Tynemouth in the year 1862, but subsequently removed to the present address, the change being necessitated by his increasing trade. The present shop is commodious and well-fitted, and in every respect adapted for the business, the position being nearly opposite the Post Office. All the usual staple kinds of fresh meat, including sound English and Scotch beef, Welsh and South Down mutton, lamb and veal in the season, with the common delicacies of the trade are supplied. Mr Champney, from his long experience, is an expert judge of sound meat, and his customers may rely on the best quality of the article being served to them. His prices are uniformly moderate, and a large and steady business is done in the town and district. All orders are punctually attended to and every satisfaction guaranteed. The excellent connection enjoyed is due to the great care with which the business is conducted and the scrupulous attention paid to the wants of customers.'*

MANOR ROAD

Situated at No 1 Manor Terrace was 'The Misses Herbert's School for Young Ladies' – situated on the corner of the present Manor Road and St Oswin's Place. In its day, it was a school of some importance, and the building exists to this day, however, it has since been renumbered and renamed as No 2 Manor Road, which in 2014 was operating as a private residential care home. A descriptive of the school premises was outlined in an 1898 guide as follows:

'The bracing air for which Tynemouth is noted, and also its excellent sanitary conditions, make it an admirable place for schools. The educational establishment of which the Misses Herbert are the principals is conveniently situated near the Railway Station and the Parish Church, the

Castle Priory and Pier being not far distant. The building is a detached house, a handsome and substantial edifice of brick, three stories in height, all the rooms and appliances of a thoroughly equipped school being provided. Young ladies are received for board and education. The principals are assisted by English and foreign governesses, and by the best visiting masters from Newcastle-on-Tyne. The course of instruction includes English in all its branches, French, German, Latin, pianoforte, violin, singing, harmony, drawing, painting, botany, needlework, dancing and drilling. There is a gymnasium in connection with the school which is a great success. The school work is regularly tested at the end of each term by an examination, and pupils are also prepared for the Cambridge Local and the College of Preceptor's examinations, as well as for the examinations of the Associated Board of the Royal College and Royal Academy of music and the Royal Society of Drawing of Great Britain and Ireland.

About eighty pupils now form the school. The references are of the best kind, including members of the nobility, the higher clergy, and many well-known gentlemen, reference being also permitted to the parents of former pupils. Full particulars may be had upon application to the principals.'

SONWIL HOUSE

Sonwil House is a large double fronted terrace property, situated on Front Street West, occupying a site to the north side of Manor Road. The house was built in 1863 and comprises three floors with stone steps leading up to an intricate carved sandstone portico exterior with turreted fasçias. A particularly unusual feature of the house is that the stonework framing every window at the front is of a different shape, as are each of the visible attic rooms. There is no specific or regular format to the exterior design and the reason for this peculiar arrangement is unknown. The name 'Sonwil' is simply an anagram of the surname 'Wilson', a former occupant of the property.

PERCY GARDENS

Commencing from the junction with Lovaine Row, Percy Gardens consists of a sweeping crescent of large Victorian houses on Tynemouth Seafront overlooking the North Sea and commanding spectacular views of Tynemouth Priory and Cliffs, King Edward's Bay and the North Pier. During the 1800s when the railway came to Tynemouth and connected a link to Newcastle, the residential popularity of the area began to grow and so plans were laid out by the Duke of Northumberland for a number of housing developments. Perhaps one of the most outstanding of these was that of Percy Gardens, which lies on the northern edge of the village.

Named after Algernon Percy, the 6th Duke of Northumberland, the street consists of a number of large residential houses with communal gardens which were once accessed by private gated driveways at each end of the road. The gardens are situated on the seaward side of the street, roughly in the shape of an oval. These gardens were originally laid out for the benefit of residents and occupiers and over the years have encompassed a bowling green, a

Above: The sweep of Percy Gardens from the south.
Below: The gated entrance to Percy Gardens from the north.

putting green, a croquet lawn, tennis courts, leisure areas, rockeries and flower beds.

A Gardener's Lodge was constructed next to the southern entrance to the street and the first live-in gardener was appointed in 1881. Responsibility for the upkeep of the lodge, road and gardens rested with each of the house owners. This involved a system of annual levies which was established under a covenant dated 1880 to meet this obligation which still remains in operation today.

During the Second World War, two Anderson shelters were accommodated in the gardens which are still in existence and the original iron railings which once surrounded the gardens were removed for the war effort but were never replaced.

Most of these houses were built during the 1870s when plots were leased to individuals who employed architects to design their houses which were independently built in a restrained Victorian style enabling a superb degree of architectural harmony. The grandeur of the houses meant that many of the first owners were recorded as affluent and wealthy men with distinguished occupations, which included Shipowners, Surgeons, Lawyers, Merchants, Engineers, Coal exporters and many others with similar professional vocations, some of whom played prominent roles in local affairs.

The sheer size of these houses dictated that nearly all households employed a number of maids and servants, and many houses remained in the same family for a number of generations.

In August 1884 HRH Albert, Prince of Wales opened the Albert Edward Dock, North Shields and disembarked from his ship on the North Pier to visit Tynemouth and the Railway Station. During his tour he was driven down Percy Gardens which was decorated with flags for the occasion, however members of the general public were not admitted to the street on this occasion.

The houses survived the decades and following the Second World War, the Duke granted freehold to the owners. As lifestyles changed significantly, a majority of these houses were converted into flats during the 1960s and 1970s which virtually trebled the number of dwellings. A few houses, however, still remain complete and intact, and many of the properties have retained their historical Victorian features such as sandstone carved porticos, intricate corniced ceilings and mosaic tiled entrance halls. At the southern end of Percy Gardens, there is a mistaken belief that Nos 7 to 12 had been destroyed in a bombing raid during the Second World War, however, this is not the case. For some unknown reason, this particular plot remained vacant and unbuilt since the beginning of the original development until a modern block of flats (Priory Court) was eventually built on the site.

Today, Percy Gardens is a thriving community of all age groups with a good community spirit. Numerous social activities for residents are organised and held throughout the year and the Percy Gardens Trust Committee work constantly to maintain the former splendour of the area. A gardener lives in the lodge situated at the south entrance to the street and is employed by the committee to care for the 3.7 acres of land there. Throughout the year, the Committee organise a variety of community events, many of which are held in the gardens.

A view across the gardens gives a spectacular view of Tynemouth Cliffs, Priory, Castle and the North Pier.

40

No 3 Lovaine Row is situated at the south end of Percy Gardens, and is incorporated in the end terrace of the street. The house has an ornately carved header stone above the door indicating; 'Percy Gardens South House'.

During the First World War, No 47a Percy Gardens (to the rear of Hope House) was under the ownership of the War Office, and used as a command centre for the coastal defences, with an observation and range-finding post built into the roof of the house to control the Tyne guns.

In 1916, a reinforced concrete tower of seven storeys was constructed to the rear of this house with rounded bay windows to the four upper floors of the south front and a small gun emplacement to the roof. This tower was designed to act as an observation post and command centre for the two 'Tyne Turrets' one of which was situated at Hartley to the north and the other at Marsden to the south. These turrets were dismantled in 1925, but the house and tower were retained until the Second World War.

In September 1938, it was apparent that war with Germany was imminent, so one of the first actions taken to prepare the Tyne for invasion was to install the fortress commander and staff officer at their offices at No 47a Percy Gardens. After the war, the site was released by the war office and the property is now part of a private residence. The tower is a Grade II listed building.

PERCY STREET

One of the largest building contractors in the Tynemouth area during the late 1800s and early 1900s was that of Mr Robert Tate. The business was conducted from premises which served as his works and offices, situated at No 54 Percy Street, Tynemouth. The workshop was adapted and fitted out with machinery for various manifold operations and an adjoining yard housed a large supply of building materials. Mr Tate was an established house builder and undertaker, who also undertook various aspects of joinery, cabinet making and upholstery as well as offering a complete funeral furnishing service.

PERCY PARK ROAD

Although Front Street was the main 'shopping' area in Tynemouth, Percy Park Road was equally as important with a small variety of shops and commercial premises which were situated nearby.

One of the earliest recorded businesses on Percy Park Road was that of Mrs Martha Mather who established her business in 1898 as a wholesale wine & spirit merchant,

with her premises being situated at 'Swiss House', No 8 Percy Park Road. 'Swiss House' still exists and was so named because of its design which has characteristics similar to that of a Swiss Chalet. In 1898, a descriptive of the business was outlined as follows:

'This establishment has already grown to considerable dimensions, the Swiss House Wholesale Wine, Spirit and Ale Stores being widely known to the trade. The premises are well suited to the character of the enterprise, and large stocks are held in all the lines dealt in. A wide selection is offered in whiskies of the finest blends, Messrs. Robertson and Sanderson's "Mountain Dew" being an important speciality.
The department of wines, including port, sherry, claret etc, of the best vintages, is particularly well supplied. In the way of malt liquors, Allsop's ales, Bass's beer, Guinness's stout, and other well-known beverages are furnished on draught and in bottle. A very full assortment of mineral waters of the best kind is also maintained. All goods are sold at town prices and delivered at the shortest notice. Orders receive careful and prompt attention in all branches, and the quality is assured as fully equal to that represented.'

By 1912, it is recorded that the premises were being run by a Mr C. Willis, and between 1920 and 1940, they were under the management of Wilkinson & Co (Spirit

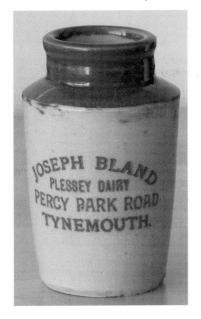

Merchants). Originally, and starting from the junction with Front Street – all premises on the east side of Percy Park Road were numeric, however between 1920 and 1928, the system changed when a renumbering system was introduced, with odd numbers being allocated to the east side of the road and even numbers to the west. As a result, these premises, which were formerly No 8, became No 23 Percy Park Road.

Another long established business was that of Joseph Bland who traded as 'Plessey Dairy'. His small shop was situated at No 11 Percy Park Road (later No 33) and is recorded in directories between 1911 and 1940.

The shop was renowned for a wide selection of dairy products, however it was particularly famed for its cream which was sold in distinctive small stoneware pots edged with the name and address in dark blue lettering. These cream pots are now quite rare and tend to command high prices amongst collectors.

Percy Park Road, c. 1928. The shop to the immediate left is that of M. Davison (Fruiterers), then J. Bland (Plessey Dairy) and H. Myers (Newsagent). Swiss House Wholesale Wine, Spirit and Ale Store is the building with the apex roof, and during this year was under the management of Wilkinson & Co (Spirit Merchants). Situated just a few doors away, at No 5 Percy Park Road another Wine & Spirit Merchant was Thomas Moore (*below right*). This shop was later re-numbered to become No 15. There have been various changes of use over the years, latterly becoming a chemist and pharmacy occupied by a branch of Boots.

A stone plaque to the side roof gable bears a date of 1897 (*below*).

The ornate three storey building on Percy Park Road, with a corner roof turret which stands at the corner of Percy Street was once a Temperance Hotel, although no record seems to appear in any old directories. This building is now No 11 Percy Park Road and has been split up and converted to private flats and apartments. The old buildings adjoining this structure incorporate an ornate date stone indicating 'Percy Buildings 1883' (*below*).

Thomas Moore,
Wine & Spirit Merchant,

5, Percy Park Road,
TYNEMOUTH.

Visitors to the coast can be assured of special attention to all Orders.

TYNEMOUTH PARK

In 1890, Tynemouth Council negotiated with the Duke of Northumberland for the lease of a plot of seven acres of land between the North Eastern Railway and the Grand Parade at Tynemouth. Three years later in 1893, Tynemouth Park was created when a new recreation ground was laid out opposite Tynemouth Palace and Winter Gardens, the focal point of which was a large pond, combined with tennis courts, bowling and putting greens plus ornamental gardens with a bandstand. The pond was often referred to as 'Tynemouth Lake' and for many years has attracted model boating enthusiasts from all over the area. In the summer of 1893 an exhibition of model yachts was held in Tynemouth Aquarium and Winter Garden. It was promoted by

TYNEMOUTH PARK.

FIVE HARD TENNIS COURTS.   THREE BOWLING GREENS.   BOATING LAKE.
MINIATURE GOLF COURSE.   PUTTING GREENS.

		s.	d.
TENNIS.	Singles, per half-hour per person		4½
	Doubles, per half-hour per person		3
MINIATURE GOLF COURSE, 9 HOLES. With use of mashie, putter and ball per round per person			3
BOATING ON LAKE.	Per half-hour per person		6
	Per half-hour, two persons		9
	Per half-hour, three or four persons	1	0
CHILDREN'S PADDLE BOATS.	Per half-hour per person		3
BOWLS.	Two players, per hour		6
	Two players, per half-hour		4
	Four players, per hour		8
	Four players, per half-hour		4
	Six or eight players, per hour		9
	Goloshes on hire, per pair		1

OPPOSITE TYNEMOUTH PARK.

PLAZA PUTTING GREEN, 18 HOLES. Per round per person		2

OVERLOOKING BATHING POOL.

SHARPNESS POINT PUTTING GREEN, 18 HOLES. Per round per person		3

REFRESHMENTS MAY BE OBTAINED AT THE CORPORATION CAFES IN TYNEMOUTH PARK AND ON GRAND PARADE.

the Tynemouth Recreation Association to encourage the sport. A Tynemouth Model Yacht Club was formed, and one of the first buildings planned for Tynemouth Park was their boat house. In 1908, rowing boats were introduced to the lake which enraged the club members so much that they called on the Duke of Northumberland's agent for aid. As a result, he forced Tynemouth Council to set aside longer hours to allow the club to have exclusive use of the lake. The first clean out of Tynemouth Lake took place in 1948, and in early in 2011, further work started in an effort to clean it up for the second time. Over the years a build-up of over 2,000 tonnes of silt promoted the growth of algae and it was necessary to call in specialist contractors to undertake the task.

Skaters assemble on a frozen lake in the park, c. 1920.

NORTHUMBERLAND PARK

During the recession of the 1880s, Tynemouth Alderman, John Foster-Spence approached the Duke of Northumberland requesting a piece of land be made available which would be suitable to be laid out as a park. His intention was to provide work for unemployed shipbuilders as well as providing a recreational facility for the residents of North Shields and Tynemouth. Accordingly, the Duke provided a large area of land between Spital Dene and Tynemouth Road and following a design by the Borough surveyor Mr Gomozinski, landscaping began in order to lay out the new park. The work included the erection of greenhouses, summer houses, aviaries, shelters and a bandstand. It was opened by The Duke of Northumberland in 1885 and named in his honour. To mark the

occasion, he planted a Turkey Oak, which was just one of many commemorative trees that were subsequently planted in the park over the years.

The townspeople were very grateful for this new facility, and this was reflected in the large number of donations that were made. Contributions included waterfowl and swans for the lake, a Silver Pheasant, an Owl and a collection of Parrots that were housed within one of the many aviaries which at one time stood here.

A delightful summary in a guidebook dated 1923 described the park as:
'A perfect paradise, with shady trees, rustic bridges, tasteful flower beds, smooth patches of turf, fragrant shrubs, well kept paths, banks on whose sides are a mass of colour in the Spring and Summer, cosy arbours, pretty ornamental lakes, and a plentiful supply of seats. There are a number of bowling greens and band performances which add to the floral attractions of this sweet spot.'

Sadly, this description is no longer applicable. Over recent years, this magnificent Victorian Park and its small lake have suffered from severe neglect and now receive only basic maintenance. The services of the permanent gardeners and park keeper have been dispensed with, and the aviaries, greenhouses, summer houses, bandstand and shelters which once adorned the area have long since disappeared. Despite this, it still remains on the 'List of Buildings and Parks of Special Local Architectural and Historic Interest'.

Over the years, much of the park has suffered from neglect, however in 2012, a Heritage Lottery Fund grant of just over £2 million has enabled restoration work to begin on returning much of this beauty spot to its former glory.

Northumberland Park in 1905.

SPITAL DENE & ST LEONARD'S HOSPITAL

Old maps indicate several variations in the spelling of Spital Dene which has also been spelled as 'Spytel', 'Spytal', 'Spitall' and 'Spittle'. A 'Spital' is an archaic name for a hospital which usually deals with contagious diseases, and in this case, Spital Dene derived its name from St Leonard's Hospital which was first referred to in an assize roll of 1293 which mentions: *'The bridge of the hospital of Saint Leonard.'*

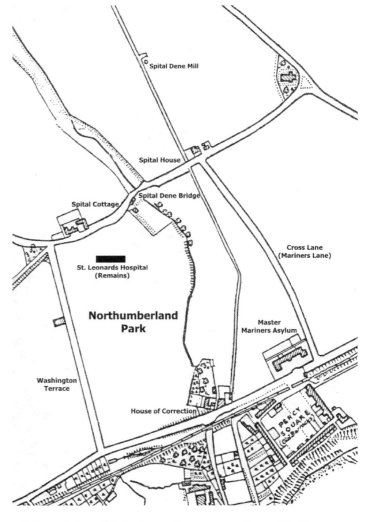

The location of the hospital does suggest it may have been a Leper Hospital because of its remote location away from Tynemouth township. Situated on the only road from Newcastle to Tynemouth, where the Prior of Tynemouth held markets on Sundays from 1275, meant there would be many people travelling across the Spital Dene Bridge. Medieval Hospitals are known to be quite commonly situated close to bridges which had important symbolic religious connotations and beggars or lepers stationed there could collect alms from all those crossing. The word 'hospital' derives from the Latin 'hospes', meaning a stranger, foreigner or guest. The original function of a hospital was to provide hospitality and shelter for travellers of all kinds, not exclusively for the sick but later a variety of institutions came into being to cater for the poor, the aged and the sick which bore the name 'hospital'.

In 1539 when Tynemouth Priory was dissolved, Spytel House and Spytal Close were surrendered to the Crown. The land was then leased to Sir Thomas Hilton by King Henry VIII for a term of 21 years. This land eventually passed to Algernon the tenth Earl of Northumberland in 1637.

Spital Dene looking west from Mariners Lane.

It was written that in 1789, the hospital ruins were still to be traced a little to the west of Tynemouth on the road to Newcastle. The old road to Newcastle went past Holy Saviour Church across the Spital Dene and along Tynemouth Old Road (once known as Cut-Throat Lane), to Preston Avenue, Preston Road and then southwards to Christ Church and from there, westwards through the village of Chirton.

The present direct road to Tynemouth was not made until after the peace of 1815. Spittle Dene Mill stood in fields to the west of Holy Saviours Church and was situated close to the present junction of Mill Grove and Dene Road from where the neighbouring streets of Millview Drive, Milldene Avenue and Millfield Grove derive their names. It is likely that the mill was used for grinding corn, however little is known of its origins and no dates are available to confirm with any certainty when it was built or demolished, however it was known to be in ruins in 1856.

The Spittle was one of the old burial places of the Parish of Tynemouth. The first two burials recorded in the Parish Register were in 1656 and 1659 being the two sons of Gabriel Coulson the Parish Clerk. In 1662, a total of 23 burials were recorded and the last recorded at this site was John Foster of Whitley in 1713/14.

When Northumberland Park was laid out in 1885 between the two branches of the Pow Burn, the foundations of a medieval building were discovered, although an excavation was not carried out far enough to discover its plan. The building appeared to be of considerable size. Its chambers were paved with stone and the few mouldings that remained were of an early English character. Some fragments of flowing window tracery, the base of a cross and the matrix were also found on the spot. The matrix is a plain limestone slab measuring 5 feet 9 inches in length and 2 feet 7 inches in breadth showing indentations which contained brasses of a layman and his wife connected by an inscription fillet. Below these two large figures are five smaller indents for the

brasses of their daughter and four sons. The male figures stand on mounds and seem to have worn long loose sleeved tunics, the two females had similar costumes, their hair curled at the side and each had a headdress covered by a kerchief. A date of between 1400 and 1420 has been assigned to the execution of the work. Two stone coffins were also unearthed in the course of the excavations and they can still be seen in the Park. In January 1968 a complete skeleton and three skulls were unearthed by Corporation gardeners near the remains of the hospital.

In 2011 as part of the heritage strategy for Northumberland Park, North Tyneside Council successfully applied for Heritage Lottery Funding to enhance the park and an archaeological survey took place to provide information for the restoration plans. In June and July that year, five trenches were dug around the known hospital remains and one on buildings known from early 19th century maps near the Spittal Bridge. Several medieval graves were uncovered and also a mixture of bones which could represent many more burials, which were probably disturbed when what was a hilly mound was levelled by the Victorians when creating the park. Also found was a considerable amount of pottery, roof and floor tiles but the most interesting finds were a 5,000 year old Neolithic stone axe and a Henry VIII silver penny circa 1520.

CLIFFORD'S FORT

North Shields Fish Quay began life in 1225 as a simple village of shielings (huts) from which the town of North Shields takes its name. The quay was originally located here to serve the nearby Tynemouth Castle and Priory. The growth of North Shields was at one time restricted due to fear that it would take trade from neighbouring Newcastle, which was the region's leading port at the time. Built to replace an earlier basic bastion of 1642, Clifford's Fort was constructed on a strategic site close to the mouth of the Tyne in 1672 to defend the river from enemy warships during the Third Anglo-Dutch War. It was named after Lord Thomas Clifford, 1st Baron Clifford of Chudleigh, was an English Statesman and politician who held a number of offices, rising to acting Secretary of State and Lord Treasurer. He served with the English Fleet, and played a prominent role during the Anglo-Dutch Wars.

Thomas Clifford (1630-73).

Clifford's Fort was crucial not just to North Shields, but also to the nation's history when it also played an important role during the later Napoleonic Wars. It was built on a raised platform and surrounded by sandstone walls with a three storey redoubt at its centre. The fort housed the governor's apartments, a gunpowder magazine and an armoury, and was protected by a low riverside gun battery.

During the 18th century, alterations were made to the fort when the eastern and southern sections of the wall were rebuilt with gun embrasures and several new buildings were added including a barracks and a master gunner's house and a ditch with a counterscarp wall constructed on the east and south sides. By 1881 the fort was declared obsolete as a place to mount guns, but suitable as a base for submarine mining.

In 1888 the fort was recommissioned as the HQ of the Tyne Division Royal Engineers (Volunteers) Submarine Miners. Most of the old buildings were demolished to make way for new structures, and the old gun emplacements were bricked up. A narrow gauge railway was laid to a gate in the southeast angle to carry mines to boats and was defended with two new gun placements. At this time more ground was enclosed in the northwest corner and boundary stones were erected to mark the forts perimeter.

In 1928 the fort was once again decommissioned and passed to the Tynemouth Corporation for the expansion of the fishing industry, however during the Second World War it was again recommissioned as an Emergency Coastal Battery. At the end of the war, the fort became redundant and was consumed by the thriving

Clifford's Fort Wall, 2011.

infrastructure of the Fish Quay and shrouded beneath fish processing facilities. It recently became a renewed source of interest during the present regeneration work.

A detailed analysis of the surviving remains allowed a clear assessment of what was significant, and revealed just how much of the fort was still intact, as well as shedding light on some later buildings important to the site's history, including two lighthouses. The full extent of the fort has only become clear in the last few years as demolition of the redundant fish processing units which covered the site from the 19th and 20th centuries progressed. Magnificent masonry forms a long low wall with 29 heavy gun emplacements facing the mouth of the Tyne. A moat and counterscarp wall has been cleared out as renovation work progresses. The surviving west and north walls, of stone rubble beneath brick parapets, with gun ports and musket loops, are probably remnants of the 1672 fort. It is now a scheduled Ancient Monument.

THE VILLAGE GREEN

Erected by public subscription and situated at the edge of the Village Green, a statue of Queen Victoria marks the patriotism of the people of Tynemouth. Designed by A.B. Plummer, and sculpted by Alfred Turner, this was only the second memorial to the late Queen unveiled in the North of England and depicts the Queen as an old woman in the midst of voluminous robes during the twilight years of her reign. The sculpture now lacks the Queen's crown and the second of two figures on each of the bosses of her throne. The remaining figure is of a mother and child. The statue was a second cast from a mould used for Turner's monument to the Queen in Delhi, resulting in a significant saving.

At a total cost of £1000, the money was collected during a time of financial strictures resulting from the Boer War. Difficulties arose in agreeing a suitable site, but eventually the Village Green was decided upon, and it was unveiled on 25th October 1902. Despite a day of heavy rain, a large crowd had gathered to witness the valedictory speech and unveiling ceremony by the Mayoress, Mrs Daglish who had been much involved in the statues fundraising. The ceremony was followed by an exhibition drill by the Tynemouth Volunteer Life Brigade, a sumptuous tea in Tynemouth Palace, a torchlight procession through the rain to the park which was followed by fireworks. By 1909, the pedestal base had been heavily stained from the bronze statue above and some preservation work was deemed necessary. The memorial was further renovated in 1994, when the statue was given a protective coating and the railings around it replaced.

The South African War Memorial, 1905.

At the opposite end of the Village Green is the South African War Memorial, constructed of red sandstone and unveiled on 13th October 1903 by the Secretary of State for War, William Brodrick in memory of those residents who were lost during the second Boer War of 1899-1902. This four-sided monument which is now severely eroded is unlike any of the usual forms associated with war memorials. The structure rises in three stages, with pilasters on each corner of the base and scrolls on each corner of the middle. A bronze plaque is attached to two of the main faces; one bears the roll of honour and the other the inscription. The boss at the top of the monument originally supported a finial.

First unveiled in 1920 to the memory of those who fell in the First World War, the centre of the green accommodates a more modern styled white granite memorial which additionally remembers those who also lost their lives during the Second World War. The front face bears a carving of a sword and wreath with an inscription below. The roll of honour is inscribed on the remaining three faces.

BUILDINGS
TYNEMOUTH PALACE AND PLAZA

One of the most prominent and majestic buildings which once stood overlooking the Long Sands at Tynemouth was doomed to failure from the day it was built. Remembered by many as simply 'The Plaza', this magnificent Victorian edifice had a chequered history.

THE NEW AQUARIUM AND WINTER GARDENS AT TYNEMOUTH

An architectural drawing of Tynemouth Aquarium and Winter Garden. The terraces and steps were never built.

Erected at a cost of £82,000 and originally known as; 'Tynemouth Aquarium and Winter Garden', the architects were Messrs John Norton & Philip Massey, of London. Construction work commenced in 1877, taking almost two years to complete. The opening ceremony was performed by Mr T. Eustace Smith MP in 1878.

The main central section consisted of two large floors, the lower one being devoted to an Aquarium, which measured 216 feet in length by 50 feet in width. It contained six fresh water and 13 salt water tanks which housed a number of aquatic specimens and were entrusted to the care of Mr Howard Birchell, the company naturalist.

Above the aquarium, the upper section formed the Winter Gardens which were of the same dimensions with a large arched glass roof supported by wrought iron framework. The building had club facilities, Pleasure Grounds, Baths, a Skating Rink, Card and Billiard Rooms with a Library containing Reading and Smoking Rooms. The building also housed management offices and bedrooms for the domestics and orderlies. With an imposing sea frontage, measuring 336 feet there was a promenade and refreshment bar towards beach-level. The north section contained the skating rink, which was capable of being flooded to provide a sea-water bathing pool.

Two 5-storey towers stood at the north and south end of the building, which were used as offices and storage areas, but also contained huge water tanks, which were designed to flood the building in the event of a fire. The architectural designs were magnificent, with plans for extensive terraces running down to beach level, but these were never started due to the enormous cost of sinking firm foundations into the sand.

In 1880, just less than two years after opening, the owners ran into financial difficulties, so the mortgage holders repossessed the building and sold it by public auction to a Newcastle company, for only £27,000 – a mere fraction of the original building costs.

In 1898, the building was re-named 'Tynemouth Palace', and by 1926 had changed its name again, this time to 'Tynemouth Plaza', however for a short time during the 1930s it was also known as 'Galaland'. During the First World War, the building was commissioned as a billet for troops. With a continued lack of support over the years, the building was sold several times, and was used as an exhibition hall, theatre, picture hall, dance hall, ballroom and skating rink.

The interior of Tynemouth Palace in 1905.

In latter years, the building fell into general disrepair, and despite efforts for revival it continued on a gradual decline. In the 1960s part of the building accommodated the 'Beachcomber Bar' and night club, followed by a partial transformation into shops, and an amusement arcade.

In the early hours of the morning on 10th February 1996, the 118 year old building was completely destroyed by a massive fire, the cause of which was never fully established but necessitated its entire demolition. A sad finale to an otherwise beautiful structure which should have really been one of Tynemouth's finest and proudest buildings.

Grand Parade and Tynemouth Palace in the early 1920s.

KNOTTS FLATS

Knotts Flats were erected on Percy Square – the former name of the area in a bay between what is known as the North Groyne and Swaddle's Hole on the north bank of the Tyne. Here, there are sloping cliffs in boulder clay reaching almost 100 feet above sea level with cliffs extending around 200 feet in width. Percy Square was originally built as barracks in 1758, and consisted of four terraces built around a parade ground overlooking the River Tyne. After the Napoleonic wars, the area was sold to the Duke of Northumberland who converted the buildings into cottages and cultivated and railed the parade ground.

In 1822, a public house by the name of the Northumberland Arms also stood on this site and was last recorded about 1861. In 1847, the northern section of Percy Square was partly demolished to accommodate the railway cutting adjacent to Tynemouth Road, between North Shields and Tynemouth.

By 1936, the area had been cleared and soon afterwards, a 1,264 foot long 'toe' retaining wall was built at the foot of the nearby cliffs to assist their stability in preparation for construction of the five storey Sir James Knott Memorial Flats. The flats were completed in 1938 to the memory of Sir James Knott with building work being financed from part of his £5,000,000 estate. The flats stretch for a distance of 750 feet and incorporate 135 homes which afford some magnificent views of the river and mouth of the Tyne. The original concept of these homes was to re-locate people who lived in overcrowded accommodation or who had no home at all, and many people were housed here following the 1933 slum clearance of North Shields Low Town.

In 1948, some serious geological problems occurred when the 'toe-wall' split into two sections; the break occurring 1061 feet from the west end, and causing the east section to move forward by a total of 4 feet, with a large tilting deformation becoming apparent immediately below the flats towards the centre section of the wall.

The problems were significant, and urgent investigations were carried out to establish the cause of the deformations and minimise the risk of slope failure which could cause collapse of the flats, endangering the large number of families living there.

It was discovered from borehole investigations, that because the toe-wall here was not grounded in rock, it had moved forward horizontally with the earth mass due to water logging of the fill material, which interrupted the natural drainage of the cliff. The toe-wall also blocked drainage by banking up the groundwater behind it. Remedial work was carried out and consisted of underpinning, reconstructing and buttressing the toe-wall, as well as draining and reshaping the cliffs to a safer profile.

Today, the flats are a landmark for many miles around.

MASTER MARINERS HOMES

There is a long maritime history associated with the River Tyne which goes back hundreds of years, and thousands of men from the surrounding area have worked on the river or have virtually lived a life at sea. It was recognised in the early 1800s that Master Mariners were generally not well provided for in their old age so in 1829 a Friendly Society was set up by a number of local Tyne Mariners in order to provide pensions and accommodation when they reached the age of 60 or became incapacitated.

Existing seafarers were encouraged to subscribe to pension funds and many local benefactors also made generous contributions to the institution's coffers.

The need for sailor's retirement homes was well acknowledged, and so the 3rd Duke of Northumberland provided a site on Tynemouth Road on which to build what was to become the Master Mariners Asylum.

Designed by architects, John and Benjamin Green, the foundation stone was laid on 18th October 1837 with construction work taking three years to complete. The total building costs were £5,100 and at the time, the structure was described as 'An excellent example of nineteenth century almshouses in a restrained but substantial style.'

Master Mariners Homes, 1907.

A clock tower was incorporated into the front of the building, beneath which a carving of the Master Mariners coat of arms can be found within a niche on the façade. A full length statue of the Duke of Northumberland occupies a position in front of the building which acknowledges his valued donation. In later years the building became better known simply as 'The Mariners Homes' which were capable of accommodating 32 aged mariners along with their dependents.

In 1902, the Society and the Tyne Mariners Institute (a pension-providing charity) were amalgamated into the present Tyne Mariners Benevolent Institution who administer the homes and provide annuities for aged and needy merchant seamen and their widows.

Today, very few of the occupants are now Master Mariners, but nearly all have been seafarers or have some previous connection with the sea. Over the years the homes have been substantially modernised and upgraded, and the Board of Trustees have a policy of refurbishing flats as they fall vacant. At one time, eligibility for a placement, required the applicant (regardless of rank or rating), to have attained the age of 55 years or be incapable of working, have served at least five years at sea or on the River Tyne and be in need, hardship or distress and residing within five miles of the River. Widows of seafarers who fit these qualifications would also be considered. The homes lend their name to the street which abuts it to the east: Mariners Lane.

TYNEMOUTH HOUSE OF CORRECTION

Following an Act of Parliament in the 18th century, an order was made to build hundreds of Correction Houses throughout England. Situated on the south east corner of Northumberland Park, next to Tynemouth Lodge Hotel, Tynemouth Correction House is one of only a few in the country still in existence. The premises were designed by a Mr William Newton, an eminent Newcastle architect, and built by Joseph Mathwin and Thomas Hutchinson for the sum of £623 6s 10d. Building plans were first put forward in 1790, and work was completed by 1792. Very little history exists in relation to the premises, but old records confirm that it was a prison for minor miscreants, such as prostitutes and petty thieves, and had holding cells for more serious offenders who were awaiting confinement at Newcastle and Morpeth County Gaol. The first Governor and Taskmaster was a former Newcastle Innkeeper – Robert Robson, who received a salary of £20 per year.

The building consisted of a Governor's house, fourteen cells, two yards, a courthouse and a shed. The courthouse itself adjoined the House of Correction immediately next to Tynemouth Lodge Hotel, separated by a narrow alleyway, and was used for dispensing justice by circuit judges and visiting magistrates who held their petty sessions there every

An old steam tram passes the House of Correction in 1904.

Tuesday. The judges and magistrates often stayed at the adjacent Tynemouth Lodge Hotel, which was built in 1799 for a Mr William Hopper, and whose cellars were once used as kitchens to prepare meals for the prisoners.

Over the years, the House of Correction has had a number of modern extensions added, however the old stone structure is still fully intact, most of which is now hidden from view behind the façade which was added in 1939 overlooking Tynemouth Road (appropriately called Correction House Bank at this location).

Notable events which occurred over the years are:

17th January 1793: A Joseph Smart was convicted of larceny, and sentenced to three months hard labour at Tynemouth House of Correction.

25th October 1809: On the occasion of the Golden Jubilee of King George III, and by order of the magistrates, all prisoners were given a good dinner and a quart of ale.

26th July 1885: A prisoner named William Daglish escaped.

2nd April 1886: A prisoner named Arthur Henderson escaped by scaling the wall of the exercise yard. He was recaptured soon afterwards.

The front gable of the old courthouse bears an old circular stone crest depicting the Castle Keep at Newcastle. By 1904, the building was no longer in use as a prison and it was suggested that the town council should buy the property for the improvement of the adjoining park, a shelter or tea rooms, however the council declined the opportunity to do so, and it was eventually taken over and converted to a laundry, in which capacity it remained for a majority of the 20th century. In the late 1960s it became the premises of an engraving and a hygiene company, when further additions and extensions were carried out and has since been used as storage, offices and a showroom for a number of small businesses. In 1999 the premises attained the status of a Grade II listed building.

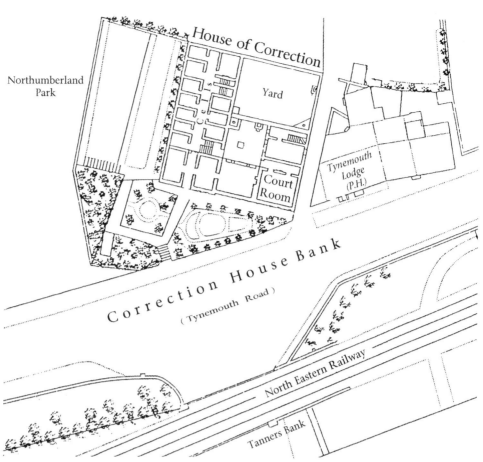

This 1858 plan indicates that Tynemouth House of Correction was once fronted by ornamental gardens.

The House of Correction in 1914, soon after its conversion to a laundry. The structure seen here is now hidden behind a façade which faces onto Tynemouth Road. Northumberland Park is to the left and Tynemouth Lodge Hotel is off camera to the right. The two female workers pictured here are Flossie and Elsie Wall.

TYNEMOUTH MANOR HOUSE

Tynemouth Manor House was a large detached building situated in its own grounds within an area of land now occupied by the present houses to the southwest side of what is now called Manor Road (formerly known as Manor Terrace), and those to the north side of Huntington Place. The grounds of the Manor House covered a triangular shape between Manor Terrace and the present railway line adjacent to Tynemouth Station with the main entrance gates facing southeast towards Front Street on the opposite side of the road from Lorne House.

Very little information is available relating to the Manor House, its early origins or occupants and it is unclear why or when it was actually built. The earliest record appears to be in Pigots Directory of 1834 when the occupant is listed as a George Weatherby. The house and grounds are also clearly marked out and shown on an 1857 Ordnance Survey map. Between 1887 and 1902 the occupant is recorded as a Mr Robert Muckle, a Land Agent to the Duke of Northumberland. By 1911 the directory listing had changed to show an R.F. Kidd (Solicitor) with the final occupant between 1920 and 1930 being an S.A. Morrison (Ship Owner).

The house eventually fell into a state of disrepair and by January 1932 proposals to demolish the building and develop the land had been submitted. A small parcel of land belonging to the North Eastern Railway Company was also incorporated within these plans. Plans for housing were presented by J.R. Wallace on behalf of three local building contractors; W. Boner, A. Park and Hastie D. Burton, and when these houses were completed, they became Nos 1 to 27 Manor Road and Nos 16 to 24 Huntington Place. A short section of the original stone wall of the manor house still remains and adjoins No 24 Huntington Place connecting to the north section frontage wall of Tynemouth railway station. Whilst Huntington Place is mentioned here, it is interesting to note that the street name is spelled two ways. The original stone plaques incorporated into the terraced houses at each end of the street show 'Huntington' whilst newer nearby plaques show 'Huntingdon'.

Tynemouth Manor House, c. 1905.

Looking northwest on Manor Terrace towards Holy Saviours Church in 1932. A signboard in the grounds of Tynemouth Manor House indicates the housing proposals.

BEACONSFIELD HOUSE

Beaconsfield House was built between 1882-84 for John Henry Burn, a coal merchant and philanthropist who inherited wealth from his father David, after making his fortune as an iron founder in Newcastle. The building, a large villa residence was for many years a prominent landmark on Tynemouth Seafront. The house and grounds covered an area of 1 acre 3 roods and was named in honour of Lord Beaconsfield (Benjamin Disraeli) who died in 1881. The property comprised a Basement, Drawing Room, Dining Room, Billiard Room, Library, eight Bedrooms, a feature staircase two indoor WCs two Bathrooms and a further three rooms for servants.

John Burn died in 1898, however his widow continued to live at the house until 1922. Between 1924 and 1945 Beaconsfield House was owned by a Robert Thornton Bolt Esq, a Provisions Importer, and there is a suggestion that it was once used as a billet for an army anti-aircraft unit during the Second World War.

By 1946, the property had been sold and taken over by Dr Barnardo's who had been looking for another home in the area to replace two of their properties which had been destroyed during wartime bombing raids. Beaconsfield House was ideal and opened in January 1946 when some boys and staff arrived late one night in the back of a lorry. This was because the local council gave Barnardo's just twenty four hours notice to either occupy the house or lose it so time was paramount. Initially, Beaconsfield House catered for twelve boys, however it had accommodation for up to forty.

In 1953, Tynemouth Council bought the house under a compulsory purchase order, following plans to develop the sea front, as a result of which on 1st September 1953 the home closed and Barnardo's vacated the property.

While the area's future was being considered, Beaconsfield House was used by other organisations, including Hexham and Newcastle Diocesan Rescue Society to provide holidays for disadvantaged children. In 1956 the council took the decision to demolish the house and this work was completed early in 1957.

Plans to build a multi-storey hotel and leisure complex were never carried forward and the site has never been developed, but still remains as a large open field which has continued to retain the popular name of Beaconsfield.

TYNEMOUTH HOUSE (KING'S) SCHOOL

King's School at Tynemouth was originally founded in Jarrow in 1860, but by 1865 had moved to its present site in Tynemouth. The school was originally known as Tynemouth House School and provided private education for local boys.

It was described in the late 1800s as: *'Conveniently situated within a short distance of the railway station and the Church of Tynemouth Priory, and though not far from the sea, it is well sheltered from the full force of the northerly and easterly winds.'*

In the 1960s the name was changed to that of King's School, and was chosen in reference to the three ancient kings buried at Tynemouth Priory: Oswin, Osred and Malcolm III. Consequently, there are many student myths as to the position of the apostrophe in the name (King's, rather than Kings').

Perhaps its most famous old boy is Stan Laurel; one half of the comedy duo Laurel and Hardy, and the Hollywood film director Sir Ridley Scott also attended this school. The school expanded and grew considerably during the latter part of the 20th century when it began to admit girls to both the Kindergarten and the Sixth Form. The school became fully co-educational in 1996, following the initial decision in 1992.

King's originally occupied a large house on Huntington Place (Tynemouth House) and the adjoining terraces. This was later extended with the addition of the Nicholson Building (Nicholson's) in the 1920s, and the Ellison Block (Ellison's) in the 1960s. Further expansion occurred in 1991 with the addition of the design, technology and art block (the Provost building.) This continued in 1999 with the addition of the Chapter Building, comprising many new classrooms, along with the lecture theatre and 700-seat King's Hall. In 2008, the school continued its development with the addition of the Oswin's building, and houses a new sports hall, dance studio, drama workshop, indoor climbing centre, a music school with recording studio, a cafeteria and all-day coffee bar, new Sixth Form study centre and social space, a new library and classrooms for English learning support, French, Spanish and PE. The building replaces the former music school, gym, changing rooms and cafeteria.

Giuseppe Garibaldi, the 19th century Italian patriot sailed into Tynemouth on 21st March 1854 and was said to have stayed at Tynemouth House whilst in exile. During his stay, a meeting was held at the house with British political and industrial leaders and he addressed them on his plans for a unified Italy. Garibaldi's portrait was painted on this visit and is now displayed in a museum in Sardinia. A blue plaque situated on the outside wall of the school building commemorates his visit, and the room where he is purported to have slept is named the Garibaldi Room.

Tynemouth House and School, 1908.

THE CLOCK TOWER

The Clock Tower and Drinking Fountain which stands at the junction of Front Street and East Street was an inspiration on the part of philanthropist and benefactor, Mr William Scott of London, who visited Tynemouth in 1860. Little is known about Mr Scott or his background, but it is known that he was a man who was so captivated by the many charms of Tynemouth and received great advantages from his stay here that he decided to commission and present the monument to the corporation for the benefit of the people of the area.

The unveiling and opening ceremony – 2nd September 1861.

Designed by Oliver & Lamb in the Venetian Gothic style of architecture, the tower combined three Clock Faces and two Drinking Fountains along with a Marine Barometer and Thermometer and was recognised as one of the most elegant designs of its day. The total design and building cost was £500. Constructed of stone and brick with alternating bands of Peterhead granite and ornate stone carvings, the pilasters support 2-centred arches over granite bowls on the north and south sides with a panelled wooden access door to the east side.

Erected and unveiled on 2nd September 1861, the east side of the tower bears the inscription: *'Erected by William Scott Esq of London, and presented to the Public, the Mayor, Aldermen and Burgesses of the Borough of Tynemouth Trustees, 1861'*, however the first part of this inscription has disappeared due to subsequent stonework repairs. The monument was designated as a Grade II Listed Building in February 1986, and underwent some essential refurbishment work in 1999. It remains as one of the most prominent and focal points in the village.

The Clock Tower in the 1960s.

THE CARLTON CINEMA

The Carlton Cinema, stood on the north side of Tynemouth Front Street. The building itself was designed by F.R.N. Haswell, a North Shields architect, and dates to September 1869 when it was originally built as a Wesleyan Methodist Chapel. As times changed over the years, the Wesleyans vacated the church, which by chance occurred at a time when small town cinemas were gaining popularity.

Front Street, Tynemouth c. 1900. The large building is the Wesleyan Methodist Chapel which was converted to become the Carlton Cinema in 1934.

The premises were purchased in 1934 by North East Cinemas De-Luxe Ltd, and underwent extensive alteration work to designs by Edwin M. Lawson of Newcastle. The façade itself was subjected to minimal external alteration work, which allowed most of the buildings original appearance to be preserved. The internal alterations, however, were quite extensive, which included the erection of a balcony with a seating capacity of 230. The stalls were designed to accommodate 500, all of which seating gave a perfect view of the 18 feet wide screen and stage.

The entrance leading to the foyer and balcony were paneled in wood, and ornamental grilles in gold were located on either side of the proscenium. The remaining décor was tastefully painted in dark red, green and fawn; the cinema was carpeted throughout and a central heating system was installed. The first resident manager was a Mr George Hill.

On Thursday 17th January 1935, the Carlton Cinema opened, and the first film shown for the opening night was *Evergreen* starring Jessie Matthews. There were 200 guests in attendance, which included Councillor Hastie D. Burton (Mayor of Tynemouth) along with his Aldermen and other distinguished guests.

Over the years, the cinema was very successful, however by 1973, the Carlton was starting to run into difficulties due to low attendance figures and a closure application was submitted to convert the building from a cinema to a bingo hall. The local authority amidst public opposition to such a change turned the application down, and in early 1976 the inevitable happened when the cinema closed. The last film shown was *It shouldn't happen to a Vet* – a film which ironically produced the best attendances for some years.

Sentiments were expressed for the need to retain a cinema, and suggestions that the local authority should take it over and perhaps include facilities for an arts centre were ruled out on the grounds of cost.

In February 1977, the council gave permission for sheltered housing to be built on the site, and so the Carlton was demolished to be replaced by Timothy Duff Court, named after a former Mayor of the town.

As many visitors and day trippers walk down Front Street towards the seafront, they may walk past Timothy Duff Court, oblivious to the fact that the now quiet site once played host to so many stars of the silver screen.

The plush foyer of the Carlton Cinema.

THE GRAND HOTEL

Overlooking the North Sea, the Grand Hotel is an imposing building situated on the corner of Percy Gardens and Hotspur Street, Tynemouth. The history of this magnificent structure goes back almost 150 years when, in 1872, Algernon George Percy the 6th Duke of Northumberland built it as a summer residence for Louisa, the Duchess, along with gardens which now form the grassed area fronting the adjacent Warkworth Terrace. The hotel was constructed in less than a year by a firm of Sunderland stonemasons with much of the stone being dressed on site.

Five years later, in 1877, it was converted to become a residential hotel and adopted the name of 'The Grand Hotel'. For many years, it has always been regarded as the most luxurious hotel in the area and is famous for its opulent 90-step sweeping staircase leading to the second and third floors, and is reminiscent of the Victorian period when such elaborate buildings officiated balls for the aristocracy.

An unusual feature of the hotel is the four-sided mansard roof, which is characterised by two slopes on each of its sides with the lower slope punctuated by dormer windows at a steeper angle than the upper. This design creates an additional floor of habitable space. In the early 1900s, the section of roof facing the seafront above the dormer windows was painted with the words 'Grand Hotel' and therefore clearly visible out at sea.

At the foot of the stairs, an ornate mahogany newel post incorporates a beautifully carved figure of lady which resembles that of a ship's figurehead and has been there since the hotel was built. The carving was originally commissioned by the

The Grand Hotel Staircase and the Carved Lady.

Duke of Northumberland and is probably a representation of his wife, Louisa, the Duchess. Until recently, the head of the carved figure was capped with a tiara, but this was damaged and later stolen.

Many well-known personalities have visited or stayed at the Grand Hotel over the years, and include actors and characters from the world of stage, cinema, politics and sport. There are few hotels in the North East that can admit to having entertained such a wide array of celebrities of screen and stage and it was quite a regular occurrence for staff to see familiar faces coming down the staircase for breakfast. A small selection of those celebrities included Mike and Bernie Winters, Stanley Baker, Margaret Rutherford and Conservative MP for Tynemouth

The Grand Hotel and nearby Hotspur Street in 1910.

Dame Irene Ward, a much celebrated visitor to the grand and noted for her variety of hats she would wear. Irish comedian Dave Allen was a guest as was also Dame Vera Lynn and yet for most people the most famous were comedy duo Stan Laurel and Oliver Hardy who would make a point of staying at the Grand hotel whenever they were appearing at the Theatre Royal in Newcastle. For Stan it was a case of coming home as he had spent an early part of his childhood living in North Shields. The hotel has survived two world wars; the 1930s depression and a constant changing of ownership and it still remains proud and majestic.

An extract from an early 1900 guidebook gives the following colourful description: *'The increasingly popular seaside resort of Tynemouth is well provided for in the way of hotels. Among which the Grand Hotel and the Bath Hotel are to be specially recommended. The Grand Hotel is a handsome and commanding structure near the famous Tynemouth Palace and directly on the sea front, enjoying to the full the fresh breezes for which the coast is noted. The arrangements and conveniences are of the most modern description, and in fact up to date in every respect.*

There is a commodious coffee-room, a handsome and spacious ballroom, a writing-room, a smoke-room, and an admirable billiard-room with a table by Burroughs and Watts. The accommodation includes thirty excellent bedrooms, and the sanitary provisions are of the best. Every endeavour is made to render the hotels really first-class family and residential establishments, personal supervision and high-class cuisine being a speciality. Residential terms are made for families and gentlemen. There is good stabling, and the postal and train arrangements are convenient in the extreme. Banquets and public and private dinners are catered for. Mr Tom Tickle, who is now the proprietor of both hotels, is well known to the general public, having lately been manager of the Grand Hotel and the Hotel Metropole, Newcastle-on-Tyne, where he gained a high reputation as a genial and attentive host.'

Tom Tickle came to the Grand Hotel in the late 1890s and was a highly respected manager, the customers liked him and it was known that he enjoyed his job. He died whilst playing billiards in the hotel with one of the locals or guests.

Tynemouth village remained a popular venue throughout the Victorian era, with tourists flocking here to indulge in its delightful climate and explore its natural beauty. Tynemouth was, for a time, a spa town and in 1912, it was recorded that the death rate in Tynemouth was the lowest in the country which was attributed to its spa water. As a result of this, such

During the First World War, the Grand Hotel was requisitioned for the use of Military Officers.

news was greeted with a huge influx of visitors. Businesses and local hotels thrived and this was the wonderful publicity needed to lure people to visit and even the Grand saw fit to advertise in the local press at the time as having 28 bedrooms, bathrooms and liveries, hot and cold water and salt supplies. Never had Tynemouth or the Grand Hotel been so busy.

Sadly the First World War took its toll on the Grand, and during 1914-18, Tynemouth village was almost overrun with young recruits billeted at nearby barracks whilst their commanding officers were comfortably accommodated in the Grand Hotel.

At that time Tynemouth village was overrun with young recruits billeted at the Barracks whilst their commanding officers were accommodated in the Grand Hotel.

The officers would indulge in heavy nights of drinking and playing billiards and when the needless war ended, the Grand Hotel simply became a mere skeleton of its former self when it was left stripped, battered and bruised after its 'military occupation'. The Grand had been left in such a state of disrepair that it had to be closed down and completely renovated and refurbished, as a result of which it did not re-open to the public until 1922. It took a lot of hard work for the Grand to become re-established and restored to its former glory with large amounts of money spent on re-decorating and repairing the damage the officers had left behind.

It is known that staff employed at the Grand always took great pride in their work. The outside entrance stairs were often scrubbed twice daily and all woodwork was polished until shining, staff would work as much as 14 hours per day, sometimes up to seven days in a row for a basic wage of just 4/- a week. The work was hard and tiring and staff were so weary after a shift that they often fell into bed out of sheer exhaustion, but it was steady employment with a roof over their heads and guaranteed food in their stomachs at a time when many other people were barely making a living.

By the 1950s the Grand Hotel was beginning to return to its former beauty after extensive restoration work had been carried out and a great deal of time and money spent by the owners.

It was also in the late 1950s, the Grand welcomed another new manager; Mr and Mrs Bright and their two young daughters from Lagos, Nigeria. Apparently Mr Bright was quite a distinguished gentleman towering over 6 feet tall whilst his wife, of welsh descendant and somewhat smaller in stature, ruled the roost with a firm hand – a compatible pair feared, yet respected. With each new manager came new ideas on how to attract more customers. It was the Bright's innovative idea to open a bar in the basement of the hotel and have it decorated by two Newcastle Art College students which at the time was

A 1920s brochure cover for the Grand Hotel.

GRAND HOTEL.

Tariff.

Terms   -   -   -   -   from 12/6 per day.
(Special Residential Terms for Winter).

Private Suites   (Comprising Sitting Room, with telephone, Two Bedrooms, Bath and W.C.)
Prices on application.

Special Week-end Terms:
Saturday Tea to Monday Breakfast   -   -   25/-

Commercial:
Bed and Breakfast   -   -   -   -   8/6
Tea   -   -   -   -   -   -   3/-
Hot and Cold Sea-water Baths and Garage—*Inclusive.*

Table d'hote Breakfast   -   -   -   -   3/-
Table d'hote Lunch   -   -   -   -   3/-
Afternoon Tea   -   -   -   -   -   1/6
Table d'hote Dinner   -   -   -   -   4/-
(Subject to seasonal alterations).

Fully Licensed.

GRAND HOTEL.

A 1930s tariff for the Grand Hotel.

considered very fashionable especially with live music at weekends. It soon became better known as 'The Troll Bar'.

Adjoining the hotel to the Hotspur Street side, was the 'Clachan Bar', which was later re-named to become 'Copperfields Bar'.

During the 1990s, the hotel came into the possession of the local Hastie family and right up to the present day, has undergone extensive refurbishment work, with vast sums of money spent in order to restore all to its former Victorian splendour. Today, the hotel consists of 40 bedrooms and an adjacent annexed house situated at No 53 Percy Gardens which provides an additional 6 bedrooms and is usually reserved for the use of long-stay guests. This house is said to be haunted by the spirit of a young girl. The story is somewhat vague, however, the young girl was supposedly called Alice, and once lived here with her parents when it is said that she died after a drowning incident – possibly in the 1920s either in the sea or open air swimming pool which stands opposite.

In the past, hotel residents staying in the annexed house have reported strange phenomena in one of the rooms which is numbered '532' and occasionally, an apparition of a young female child has been sighted on the nearby staircase.
Over the years, a regular visitor to the Grand Hotel who had often stayed in room 532, reported that on several occasions his wristwatch has been moved from his bedside table to another part of the room whilst he was asleep overnight. At first, he thought perhaps a member of the hotel staff had entered his room and moved the watch, but enquiries confirmed that this was definitely not the case. This seems to happen on a regular basis and, in each instance, the watch is mysteriously moved to one of several other places within the room. Apparently, Alice had a particular fascination with her father's pocket watch which he had lost, and therefore the incidents are possibly connected.

Other unexplained occurrences in the house involve bedside lamps being mysteriously switched on and off and furniture being moved. The 'ghost' however, appears to be quite friendly, and despite extensive research, no other tangible information seems to be available.

This early 1930s image shows members of Tynemouth Borough Police Force outside the Grand Hotel which was probably posed after an Annual Inspection of the Force.
To the front row, the Chief Constable, Tom Blackburn sits beside Alderman Richard Irvin.

CHURCHES & CEMETERIES
HOLY SAVIOURS CHURCH

The foundation stone of Holy Saviours Church was laid in September 1839, and the church now occupies a prominent position at the corner of the Broadway and King Edward Road, Tynemouth. It is the only church in Tynemouth belonging to the Church of England. The parish presently covers an area of 730 acres, from Northumberland Park in the southwest to Beach Road in the north.

Designed by architects, John & Benjamin Green of Newcastle, the site was donated by the Duke of Northumberland along with the sum of £200 towards building costs which totalled £2,500. Construction work began in September 1839, with the foundation stone being laid by Mr Matthew Bell MP. The chapel was 83 feet long, 41 feet in breadth and originally had a 95 foot high spire with wooden framework which surmounted a stone tower at the west end.

During 1936, concerns were expressed over the structural condition of the spire, which worsened during the Second World War as a result of heavy vibrations from nearby Anti-Aircraft guns. The War Damage Commission paid for its removal in 1949 and it has never been replaced.

Holy Saviour's Church in the 1920s, showing the original spire.

The first service took place on 18th April 1841, however the church was not consecrated until 11th August that year. Bishop Edward Malby presided during the ceremony and the building was opened as a chapel of ease to Christ Church North Shields. The Vicar of Tynemouth (of Christ Church North Shields) was responsible for the services, although in 1846, Rev George Latimer (curate), was in immediate charge. During the first twenty years of the chapel's existence, the Church of England became increasingly aware of the need for greater accommodation and free pews, otherwise membership would be predominantly upper and middle class, and the poor would have no place to go. Tynemouth's church was built prior to 1851, when it was estimated that less than 20% of the urban population could have been accommodated, so Holy Saviours Church was required to serve the inhabitants of Tynemouth parish from the mouth of the Pow Burn by the Fish Quay and as far north as Earsdon.

In April 1861 by order in council, Holy Saviours was formally separated from the mother church of Tynemouth (Christ Church) and described as 'The District Chapelry of Tynemouth Priory'. The new living had previously been offered by the Duke of Northumberland to the Rev Thomas Featherstone on 21st November 1860.

Over the years, the church has gone from strength to strength and still plays a strong role in Tynemouth. Eleven incumbents have followed the footsteps of Thomas Featherstone, along with the assistance of 21 curates.

TYNEMOUTH CONGREGATIONAL CHURCH

'Separatists' first emerged in the late 16th century in small, short-lived associations, also known as 'Independents'. Because authority lay with the congregation, and not with the ministers, it came to be known as 'Congregationalism'. Each congregation was a 'gathered Church', which organised itself independently of all external influences.

Designed by Newcastle architect Thomas Oliver, Tynemouth Congregational Church is a fine Gothic style building which stands proudly on the corner of Front Street and Colbeck Terrace, towering over all the adjacent buildings.

Front Street in 1904. The Congregational Church almost dominates the view.

Construction work commenced in 1865, and took three years to complete, with the official opening taking place on 3rd June 1868. With a seating capacity of 500, it catered for the villagers and the increasing numbers of tourists

It was not until the winter of 1873/74 that the 180 foot high spire was added at an additional cost of £1,250. Further expansion in 1884 saw the purchase of two houses adjoining the church which allowed for conversion to a church hall. Most of the stone was cut on site, and is reflected in the superb architecture of the entire building, and rare stone gargoyles are apparent near the gable corners of the spire. A large stained glass memorial window was added in 1903 to the honour of a Mr Francis C. Marshall, who was a much esteemed member of the church for many years.

By 1954, falling membership led to a covenant with the Methodist Church in Front Street and when the Methodist premises were sold, the united congregation met in the Congregationalist buildings. The Church was finally dissolved on 30th June 1973, and care of its members entrusted to St Columba's United Reformed Church in North Shields. A reorganisation of the local circuit provided for the absorption of the Methodist members into the relatively new Cullercoats Methodist Church.

The Church and buildings were eventually sold, and in 1980 were converted to become 'The Land of Green Ginger' Shopping Mall and the United Reformed Galleries. Other parts of this fine Grade II listed building have since accommodated a pub and bar, and a restaurant.

A view of the Congregational Church from Colbeck Terrace in 1909.

ST OSWIN'S CHURCH

Although no date is evident, St Oswin's Church once stood close to Pier Road and was originally a small tin chapel of worship of which the site is indicated with an inverted 'V' mark on a nearby house. The present small and spireless church however, is virtually hidden away from view and set back from the road on the south side of Tynemouth Front Street. It was designed by Newcastle architects, Hansom & Dunn and built in 1890 in a traditional east/west configuration in its own grounds and fronted with a walled garden. Although usually shortened to 'St Oswin's' the full and correct name for the church is Our Lady & St Oswin's RC Church.

The foundation stone was laid on 8th September 1889, and the church was opened on Trinity Sunday, only nine months later. The Parish Priest at this time was Canon George Howe who was also a very talented musician. The name of St Oswin was chosen for the church in tribute to Oswin, King of Northumbria who was buried in the nearby Priory grounds.
The Priory once owned this title, but at the Reformation it became vacant with the suppression of the monastery in 1539 and so the title was taken up for the church and parish, so that the traditions of the Priory and its monks could be continued in service to God and neighbours.

Unusual for a church of this era, there are strong iron trusses which support the roof timbers. During the Second World War, this construction method was to the advantage of the church, which in April 1941 suffered damage following an air raid attack when a German bomber dropped a sea mine (intended for the river mouth), which exploded on the nearby Pier Road and causing extensive damage to neighbouring property. Fortunately, the church remained relatively unscathed.

PRESTON CEMETERY

Prior to 1856, the burial ground of Tynemouth Priory and Christ Church at North Shields were used for internments. Many other burials also took place at the North Shields and Tynemouth General Cemetery situated on Albion Road, however as the population increased, church graveyards were beginning to pose serious health risks due to 'overcrowding', as space became limited for future burials.

The Burial Acts of 1852 and 1853 enabled local authorities to administer their own cemeteries and Parish vestries elected Burial Boards to manage them, and so in March 1855, Tynemouth Council met to consider the purchase of a site in Preston Township as a new burial ground. An agreement was reached and 28 acres of land was purchased from local landowner, Mr John Fenwick of Preston House for £4,200.

The new grounds were quickly laid out to incorporate wooded walkways, and the main entrance was built on the present day Walton Avenue. This included two large ornate stone pillars which house iron gates and enclosure railings next to a stone built lodge. A second lodge stands at the north entrance next to the old path of White House Lane. Two mortuary chapels were also constructed; an Anglican Chapel to the north side, and a Non-Conformist Chapel to the south side which are separated by the main driveway and bounded by a formal arrangement of laurel hedges. Both Chapels are still in regular use, however in 1959, the Anglican Chapel underwent alteration work, to incorporate modern crematorium facilities to the rear.

The oldest sections of the cemetery grounds include numerous mature trees, many of which were planted during the 1800s. The entire area also offers an important home and shelter to a variety of plants and wildlife. The grounds are rich in history with the oldest gravestones dating back over 300 years. These are situated close to the boundary wall at the back of Hazel Avenue and were brought to Preston Cemetery from Cullercoats in 1872.

One of the many memorials in the grounds was erected as a tribute to the 26 lives that were lost when the SS *Stanley* was wrecked in a storm at the entrance to the River Tyne in 1864 *(Roundabout Tynemouth – July 2010)*.

Other headstones of significance are scattered throughout the cemetery grounds including 152 First World War burials. A Second World War plot contains 223 burials, which includes 26 men

The unaltered South (Non-Conformist) Chapel in the grounds of Preston Cemetery.

from the HMS *Patia* which was sunk off the Farne Islands following an air attack in April 1941. Some of these come under the auspice of the Commonwealth War Graves Commission. Dozens of other old headstones scattered throughout the grounds bear interesting local names and inscriptions.

Preston Cemetery was first opened in 1856, and is still one of the largest open spaces in the North Shields area.

Walton Avenue looking south from Preston Village. The northern edge of the cemetery wall is visible to the right.

THE RAILWAY

Designed by Benjamin Green, the first railway station to be built in Tynemouth was constructed at Oxford Street during the 1840s for the Newcastle & Berwick Railway Company. The first train departed from there in the early hours of the morning of 31st March 1847, carrying commuters and passengers to Newcastle. The station was the terminus of an extension beyond the North Shields terminus which opened in 1839. The station had three platforms, two of which were open to the elements until the 1860s when glazed ridge-and-furrow roofing was added by the North Eastern Railway to incorporate a degree of shelter and comfort to passengers. The station building itself stood at right angles to the end of the lines beyond the buffer-stops. It contained the

Oxford Street Station in 1956 when it was in use as a goods depot. The structure still remains, and is now incorporated into the modern housing development forming part of 'Mariners Point'.

stationmaster's accommodation and offices, and entry to the booking hall and platforms was through the main gothic style portico beneath the projecting central gable and by 1850, a railway hotel known as the 'Royal Hotel' had also been constructed beside the south departure platform.

Including Oxford Street, Tynemouth over the years, has been home to a total of five railway stations, three of which were built between 1860 and 1865. In 1882, the fifth station was built. It was the huge Victorian Structure which most people now know and recognise on Station Terrace. When this new station opened on 7th July that year, Oxford Street became redundant as a passenger station, but remained in use as a goods depot until March 1959. It was then vacated to become a coal depot which stood until the

Oxford Street Terminus, c. 1905.

1970s before being abandoned completely and falling into disrepair; however it was later given listed building status before being incorporated into the modern sheltered housing development now called Mariners Point.

The nearby hotel was converted to offices and eventually fell derelict to be demolished in the 1980s.

The second station, built by the Blyth and Tyne Railway Company was situated on the north side of Tynemouth Road, between Northumberland Park and the Master Mariners Homes. It was known as the North Shields terminus. This was primarily a goods station which opened in 1860; however it assisted with a passenger service between 1861 and 1863. It later continued in use and served as a goods station and coal sidings for over a century before full closure in 1971. The site was cleared and is now occupied by residential housing known as Hazeldene Court.

One of the 1860s Goods Stations built by the Blyth and Tyne Railway Company. The building was situated between Tynemouth Lodge Hotel and the Master Mariners Homes.

The year 1863 saw the opening of the third station which was situated immediately to the west of Mariners Lane, near to the junctions of Beanley Crescent and Shipley Road. A cycle path from Mariners Lane runs through the station site and degraded remains of the station platforms are still discernible. Little else is known of the station or building which was closed in 1882.

In 1865, the fourth station was constructed for the Blyth and Tyne Railway Company and was opened on a new alignment of the former (Mariners Lane) station, on the north side of Tynemouth Road between Mariners Lane and Station Terrace terminating in what is now the TA centre. This station was short-lived and closed in 1882 following which it was demolished soon after the present day (fifth) railway station was built.

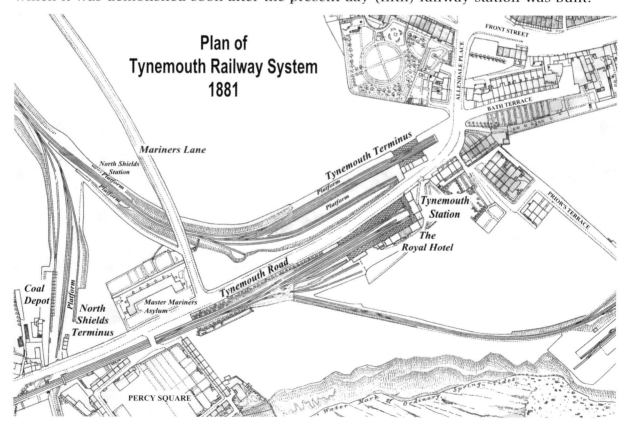

The present Tynemouth Station

In 1864, all the railway lines at Tynemouth were taken over by the North Eastern Railway Company who set about building the present loop line from Newcastle to the coast. The huge newly constructed railway station fronting onto Station Terrace was the result of a partnership between Mr Thomas Elliot Harrison who was an engineer to the North Eastern Railway, and Mr William Bell, who in 1877 became chief architect to the North Eastern Railway.

This station was a magnificent showpiece for the North Eastern Railway which opened on 7th July 1882 and was designed to handle large volumes of excursion traffic as well as the regular train services from Newcastle.

The volume of passengers in 1911 is reflected in statistics which indicate that a total of 356,302 tickets were issued at this station during that year.

The splendour of the station was noted by many visitors to the area and a description recorded in 1900 states: *'This building is without doubt the prettiest station of any large town in this country with its charming beds of flowers, its pendants of floral beauty covering its roof and hanging all over its supporting pillars.'*

Between 1900 and 1910, the staff received First, Second and Special prizes in the North Eastern Railway best kept station competition, and this tradition continued for a number of years afterwards.

Tynemouth Station in its Heyday, with its beautiful floral arrangements.

On the Station Terrace side, the external façade of the station was articulated into three blocks with a cantilevered glazed central awning, which has been renewed in recent years.

Internally, the station comprised a very large passenger circulating area and concourse. The south wing comprised separate waiting rooms (first and second class) with ladies' toilets, a booking office and hall, a general waiting room and a first class men's waiting room. The north pavilion comprised gentlemen's toilets (shared by first and second class), a telegraph office, a porter's room and the stationmaster's office, all of which featured detailed and intricate windows and doors. Over the years however, a number of changes were made to the station layout as various offices and waiting rooms were rearranged to accommodate booking and parcel offices etc.

There were two extensive through platforms for regular rail traffic, and six bays with separate platforms for excursions and goods, all of which were almost completely covered by 25 bays of ridged and glass roofing.

Much of the elaborate design work and supporting pillars are mildly gothic in style with light iron scrollwork to the roof trusses.

A unique feature of the station was the provision of a composite bridge comprising two internal passenger footbridges which flanked a central luggage corridor, which was accessible by hydraulic lifts that were powered by an accumulator in a brick tower which still survives at the rear entrance of the station. The lifts however have long since been dismantled.

A tiled wall map of the railway system has survived the decades on the interior north wall of the east concourse and the station clock is sited above the main entrance in an ornate stone surround.

Above: Horses and fishcarts queuing outside the goods platform door at the southern extremity of the station building, c. 1899.

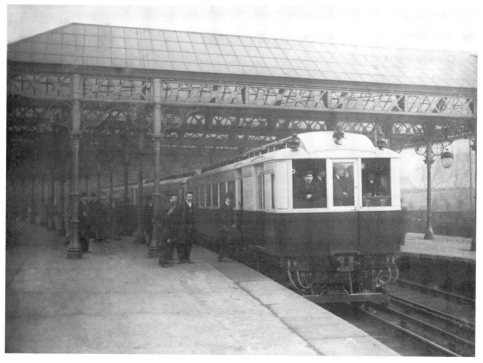

Right: An early electric Train at Tynemouth, c. 1915.

Throughout the Victorian and Edwardian days, thousands of day trippers flocked to the coast, but eventually a decline set in after nationalisation of the railways.

The goods section of the station closed in March 1959 and in 1967, the electric trains were replaced with slow and unpopular noisy diesel units. The railway had now almost reached the end of its life, until the coming of the Metro system in August 1980, when the lines were re-electrified to combine a fast and efficient service to Newcastle and beyond. Sadly, the system no longer required such a huge station; much of which by then had fallen into a state of disrepair, however it is a building of national importance, having attained Grade II listing status in 1978, and a more appropriate and commercially profitable use was needed for its vast 'greenhouse' interior.

An innovation was the launching of a weekend market, held on the concourse, which has brought a large space to life in a way comparable with the busy excursion days of the Victorian period.

Following the presentation of a feasibility study by Community Service Volunteers in 1986, a voluntary group called Friends of Tynemouth Station was formed the following year to see how the station could be saved and as they became an important community resource, the group succeeded in changing official attitudes, at the same time enlisting widespread support. Then funding was secured to carry out the first part of the restoration which restored the canopy over the west platform and over the central part of the east concourse. All the buildings on the east and west sides were restored for commercial use. The bridge was completely renovated, with the central section being opened up to become an exhibition space.

Commencing in 2011, the final phases of the restoration on the east side, part funded by a Sea Change grant and English Heritage, dealt with the outer sections of the platforms and canopy, thus revealing the full size of the station.

The building is one of national importance and is now Grade II* listed. It is gradually being brought back to life through various funding elements. The Friends support these objectives and continue to promote the station. Various activities and events illustrate the important role that this wonderful building can have in the 21st century, and to think it could have so easily been lost!

Since 1993, the Friends of Tynemouth Station have organised book fairs (originally with the Library Service) that have proved very successful. Held four times a year, the fairs attract book dealers and collectors from all around the country. To celebrate the book fairs' 20th anniversary, organiser Ylana First was presented with a stone book to recognise her work. The book sculpture was created by book seller and stone mason Gert van Hoff. Ylana, who lives in Tynemouth, helped set up the Friends of Tynemouth Station and is still heavily involved. As well as the book fairs, since 1995 over 45 exhibitions of art work have been displayed in the Bridge Gallery in the centre of bridge. Events such as these are fully supported by the station's owners – Station Developments Ltd. In 2007 Ylana was awarded the MBE for services to the station and the arts in North Tyneside.

PEOPLE

HARRIET MARTINEAU

Harriet Martineau was born at Norwich on 12th June 1802 and was an English writer and philosopher who was renowned in her day as a controversial journalist, sociologist, political economist, abolitionist and life-long feminist. The sixth of eight children, Harriet Martineau was intelligent, but weakly and unhappy; she had no sense of taste or smell, and moreover grew deaf while young, having to use an ear trumpet. At the age of sixteen the state of her health and nerves led to a prolonged visit with relatives in Bristol where her life became happier. From 1819 to 1830 she again resided chiefly at Norwich and at the age of twenty her deafness became confirmed. In 1821 she began to write anonymously for the *Monthly Repository* a Unitarian periodical, and in 1823 she published *Devotional Exercises and Addresses, Prayers and Hymns.*

In 1826 her father died, leaving a bare maintenance to his wife and daughters. Harriet then had to earn her living, and, being precluded by deafness from teaching, took up authorship in earnest. She wrote stories and in 1830 was awarded three essay prizes of the Unitarian Association.

From 1831 she wrote a series of tales designed as *Illustrations of Political Economy*, followed by two novels; *Deerbroke* and *Maid of all Work,* the sale of which was enormous, after which her literary success was secured. In 1839, Harriet's health broke down when she developed a chronic illness, as a result of which she stayed with her brother-in-law, a Newcastle physician to receive treatment for her symptoms. After hearing her friends talk about Tynemouth's fine bracing air, its old romantic history natural charm and quietude, Harriet decided to move to the village and took up residence at a lodging house, owned by a Mrs Halliday at 57 Front Street. This was on 16th March 1840.

Harriet had expected to remain an invalid for the rest of her life and delighted in the freedom her telescope allowed as she looked over Priors Haven, the Headland and across the river, all of which painted a lyrical picture of Tynemouth.

Harriet remained at 57 Front Street for nearly five years where she produced some of her best books and novels which included: *The Hour and the Man, The Prince, Settlers at Home, Feats on the Fiord and The Crofton Boys.* Another book entitled *Life in the Sick-Room* describes her life in Tynemouth. She also devoted several pages of her autobiography to this period.

Early in January 1845, Harriet left Tynemouth almost fully restored to good health and moved on to Ambleside, building a house named 'The Knoll' where she died on 27th June 1876, some 30 years later.

57 Front Street at Tynemouth is a Grade II listed building, constructed in the mid 1700s as a Georgian Town House which has since been converted to a family-run Guest House and is marked with a plaque above the adjacent archway outlining Harriet's period of residence there.

PRESS GANGS

During the French Wars at the end of the 18th century, North Shields and Tynemouth were regular victims of Press Gang raids which were once a common occurrence on the North Eastern coast. Tyneside suffered particularly badly from the Press Gangs, because of its large community of seamen and its reputation for the skilled boatmen of North Shields and the keelmen of Newcastle. It is recorded that on 26th April 1793, troops from the Tynemouth garrison took the exceptional precaution of drawing a cordon around North Shields while the Press Gangs from warships in the harbour rounded up no less than 250 seamen, mechanics and labourers and pressed them into service here. One of the naval vessels involved in such Press Gang raids, *The Peggy* is remembered in the name of 'Peggy's Hole', situated by the River Tyne near to North Shields Fish Quay.

Press Gangs were greatly feared on Tyneside, as once a man had been unwillingly pressed into naval service, his wife and family would have to rely on the local parish for support. Indeed the Poor Rate in those districts of Tyneside with large communities of seamen and boatmen rapidly increased following Press Gang raids. Because of their importance to the national coal industry the keelmen of Newcastle were supposed to be exempt from the Press Gangs but in reality, they did not escape the naval raids. In particular, the residents of Sandgate, Newcastle, which was home to many of the keelmen lived in constant fear of the Press Gangs of a certain Captain Bover whose men operated regularly and harshly on the Newcastle quayside:

Here's the Tender comin', Pressing all the men,
Oh dear hinny, what shall we dee then.

Here's the tender comin', Off at Shields Bar,
Here's the tender comin', Full of men o' war.

They will ship yer foreign, that is what it means,
Here's the tender comin', full of Red Marines.

So hide me canny Geordie, hide yorsel' away,
Wait until the frigate makes for Druridge Bay.

If they tyek yer Geordie, whes te' win wor breed?
Me and little Jacky would better off be deed.

Impressment refers to the act of taking men into a navy by force and without notice. It was used by the British Royal Navy from 1664 and continued throughout the 18th and early 19th centuries, usually in wartime, as a means of crewing warships.

The Royal Navy impressed many merchant sailors, as well as some sailors from other nations. People liable to impressment were '*Eligible men of seafaring habits between the ages of 18 and 45 years*'. It is known that non-seamen were impressed as well (particularly vagrants), although this was uncommon. Impressment was strongly criticised by those who believed it to be contrary to the British Constitution at the time. Unlike many of its continental rivals, Britain did not conscript its subjects for any other military service other than a brief experiment with army impressment from 1778 to 1780. Although the public opposed conscription in general, impressment was repeatedly upheld by the courts, as it was deemed vital to the strength of the navy and, by extension, to the survival of the realm.

After the Napoleonic Wars, in 1814 the Royal Navy fought no other major naval actions again and so ended the practice of impressment until a century later when, at the outbreak of the First World War, conscription was introduced for all the military services.

ADMIRAL LORD COLLINGWOOD

Admiral Lord Cuthbert Collingwood, the son of a merchant was born in Newcastle on 26th September 1748. After being educated at the city's Royal Grammar School, he joined the Navy in 1761 when he was just 12 years old. He sailed out of the Tyne on board the *Shannon*, a frigate on which he was to learn the rudiments of seamanship.

By 1772, Collingwood had became an experienced seaman, and by 1777 he first met Lord Horatio Nelson, then a midshipman which sparked the start of a life-long friendship in which both men were set to rise through the ranks.

Lord Collingwood's promotions were earned as he was pitched into a number of encounters through the American War of Independence and the Napoleonic Wars and it was whilst he was Nelson's second in command at the Battle of Trafalgar that he achieved his greatest notoriety, both as master of his ship the *Royal Sovereign* and by taking command of the British Fleet during the battle whilst his friend and Commanding Officer lay mortally wounded.

The Battle of Trafalgar has always been inextricably linked with the name of Lord Nelson, however Collingwood's involvement and contribution was immense. On 21st October 1805, the combined forces of France and Spain were crushed by the English fleet, and had the Royal Navy lost the battle, Napoleon with his 115,000 troops based at Boulogne, would have swept across the channel and invaded England.

Collingwood's commitment to the Royal Navy's supremacy didn't stop in battle. When he was back at home, Collingwood planted acorns at every opportunity to boost future stocks of oak timber for British ships.

After his famous victory, he received a pension of £2,000 per annum and was awarded a peerage. He died at sea off the coast of Menorca on 7th March 1810 and was later buried in St Paul's Cathedral, alongside his close friend, Lord Nelson.

In 1845, a statue of the great man was erected in his honour, and marked Collingwood's family connection with the River Tyne and Tynemouth. The statue, which was sculpted by John Graham Lough and designed by John Dobson, celebrates his life and achievements and is prominently positioned, with Lord Collingwood staring out to sea, his hand resting on a rope wrapped bollard. The figure is 23 feet tall and stands on a massive base incorporating a flight of steps and flanked by four cannons from his flagship – *Royal Sovereign* which were added to the monument in 1849.

On 7th March 2010, the 200th anniversary of Collingwood's death was commemorated in Tynemouth which included cannons from the Admiral's Trafalgar flagship, *Royal Sovereign*, being 'fired' – using pyrotechnics – to signal the start of a remembrance service.

These cannons were last fired in battle on board Collingwood's vessel, *Royal Sovereign* as it led British ships in 1805. There was also an exchange of gun salutes between the visiting Royal Navy ship, HMS *Cumberland* as well as Army field guns on shore.

MATTHEW AUTY

Born in 1850, Matthew Auty was the son of a Yorkshire joiner who became a tobacconist. In 1879 he is recorded as trading from premises on Tynemouth Place and old directories indicate his residences were at No 18 Edith Street, Tynemouth in 1880, No 9 Latimer Street in 1886 and No 17 Percy Park Road in 1887.

Auty dabbled in photography, and in 1883 he gave up his trade as a tobacconist when he acquired and opened up a photographic studio at No 20 Front Street, Tynemouth. The premises consisted of a reception room, studio and dressing rooms on the ground floor, whilst the upper floor of this and the adjoining premises (No 21) were used as workrooms where staff were later employed and dedicated to the finishing and touching-up of portraits and the production of enlargements and photographic plates.

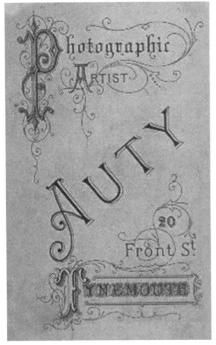

Above: Front Street, Tynemouth c. 1900, showing Matthew Auty's studio to the left.

The general management of the business eventually came under the direction of a Mr Harry Simmons, and a beam in the attic processing room carried the names of many of his other staff members which included some well known photographers such as Gladstone Adams, James Cowie, William Henry Elliott and Burton Graham.

The studio which was described at the time as: *'The largest and best lighted in England'*, was extremely successful and his photographic views and images of the coast and surrounding countryside soon became popular.

Matthew Auty plied his trade producing Studio Photographs, Stereoviews and Cartes-de-Visite, as well as Collotype and Platinotype Prints and 'Shilling View' Albums.

Left: The typical reverse side of a Victorian Carte-de-Visite or studio photograph produced by Auty.

The interior of Auty's Studio, c. 1900.

Auty claimed to have been the first to introduce the Continental idea of picture postcards to the North of England where many of Auty's views familiarised prospective visitors with the charms of the area. As the popularity of Picture Postcards began to grow, he began to specialise in the production of views of the North East of England, travelling all over the coastal and rural areas of Northumberland, and often as far afield as Cumberland, Yorkshire and the Scottish Borders to capture interesting scenes.

Each postcard in his series was numbered to identify the image and location, and over the years he produced many hundreds of different views, all of which have become very collectable. Auty photographed many static street scenes because in the early days of photography when film speeds were very slow, photographing moving people usually resulted in a blurred image.

For many years Matthew Auty was an officer of the Northern Counties Photographic Association, and was held in high esteem for his skill and knowledge, and his willingness to pass it on.

He died on 29th July 1895 aged just 45 years, and the business passed to a Mr Godfrey Hastings who commissioned his own business but retained the respected name of Auty. From 1930, the entire business transferred next door to No 21 Front Street and is still listed there in directories dated up to 1958, but from here, the business seems to have disappeared back into history. During its time, the business was extremely successful, however it has never been established what happened to the vast collection of plates and negatives from which much of Auty's work was produced.

A picture postcard in the Auty Series showing Saville Street, North Shields.

SIR JAMES KNOTT

Sir James Knott was a very successful and prominent local businessman who was born on 31st of January 1855, at Howdon on Tyne. The son of Matthew Knott, a grocer, James was the eldest of ten children. He was educated in North Shields, leaving school at the age of 14 years to start work as an office boy in a shipping office on Newcastle Quayside. James was an ambitious young man, who was intent on setting up in business as a shipbroker. At the age of 19 years, he borrowed £500 to finance his venture, and he purchased his first vessel; an old collier brig, called the *Pearl* for £186, and this was just the start of his wealth and fortune.

In 1878, he married his wife Margaret Annie, and had three sons: Thomas Garbutt Knott, Major James Leadbitter Knott and Captain Henry Basil Knott (the latter two being killed in action during the First World War).

In 1881, Sir James purchased his first steam ship the *Saxon Prince*. By 1883 he added a further 8 steam ships and by 1886 had a fleet of 17 vessels.

Sir James qualified as a barrister in 1889, and he practiced for about 4 years before returning to his love of shipping, meanwhile, he was a JP for Northumberland. In 1895 he set up the Prince Line Ltd, which went on to be the third largest privately owned shipping line in the world. In 1897 it became the Prince Steam Shipping Association and by 1898 he had a fleet of 35 vessels trading all over the world. In 1914 this had increased to 45 vessels, 32 of which were built in Tyneside shipyards. His business was managed from offices in Milburn House, Newcastle. By 1914 Sir James Knott held a commission in the Royal Navy Reserve, but was never called up, as his shipping expertise was so important to the war effort. Two years later, in 1916 his shipping empire was sold for £3,000,000 to the Furness Withy Co. Other business interests included Togston Colliery (later the Acklington Coal Company & Broomhill Colliery). He also had stakes in the South Wales Primrose Coal Company anthracite mine.

A philanthropist and a Knight of Grace of the Order of St John of Jerusalem in England, he was created a Baronet in 1917. His Coat of Arms bore the words 'Facta non Verba' which translates into, 'Deeds not words'.

By 1918, Sir James also had property interests in Heddon village including East Town Farm, Clayton Terrace, Blue Row, Garden House, the Blacksmiths shop and the Three Tuns Inn. He was described as a strong, genial, vigorous, enthusiastic and courageous man. He was noted to have a retentive memory and very observant. He was a regular attendee at church and an ardent Conservative.

In 1924, Sir James purchased Samares Manor on the island of Jersey, and retired there with his wife, Margaret Annie. He died there on 8th June 1934, aged 79 years. The bulk of his £5,000,000 estate was left to create the Sir James Knott Memorial Trust Fund, and in recognition of his work the Sir James Knott Memorial Flats were erected in 1938 with part of those funds.

The Knott family was great benefactors to the North East and in particular to the village of Heddon on the Wall, where they had a major influence on the village. The Memorial Park which opened in 1925, was created in memory of Sir James Knott's two sons who were both killed in action in the Great War.

In 1936, Sir James Knott's son, Sir Thomas Garbutt Knott, who had inherited his father's title, gave to the village of Heddon, the Knott Memorial Hall in memory of his father and mother. Apart from the well known 'Knott's Flats', the Knott family has also been responsible for numerous charitable works close to home, including the Sir James Knott Nursery School, on River View, Tynemouth, the Sir James Knott Youth Centre (YMCA) which opened in North Shields in 1938 and the RNLI Lifeboat, the *Sir James Knott* which was built in 1963, and based at Cullercoats until 1969.

CONSTABLES' COURAGE

It could be reasonably assumed that the evening of 22nd April would be tranquil with perhaps a balmy breeze blowing across the mouth of the Tyne. In most years this would be the case but not in 1939!

The threat of uncertainty in Europe was high, political storms were brewing and the threat of hostilities was uppermost in the minds of people. However, that evening the thoughts of the ten man crew of the Cullercoats lifeboat *Richard Silver Oliver* were on another matter, that of rescue.

They had been called to a rescue in the troubled, raging coastal waters. The storms brewing in Europe had transferred to the sea, and the rescue of distressed sailors was to them at that moment, far more important than the threat of war.

Disaster struck. The lifeboat capsized and in the process the crew members were themselves in danger. History tells us that six of those members, to whom the word bravery was not important, lost their lives in the unleashed torrents of what would be expected to be calmness at that time of year.

The alarm was raised and the rescue services called to the scene, just off Sharpness Point. At that time the Police controlled Fire and Ambulance activities as well as normal constabulary duties, thus two constables, PC's Fred Millions and James William Carss rushed to the scene. What lay before them was obvious, lifeboat men were strewn in the water, some showing signs of life, others not. Without hesitation and with no thought of their own safety, both constables discarded their heavy clothing and entered the water, swimming out to the upturned vessel. How they survived in the conditions is beyond comprehension, but survive they did, between them rescuing four crew members from the raging sea. Exhausted, there was little else they could do.

Lifeboat House, Cullercoats.

Cullercoats Lifeboat House in the 1930s.

On being appointed, Police Officers are sworn to serve the public in many ways, not least in preserving life. This was the case that night and in consequence both officers were later presented with inscribed silver watches, the Silver Tynemouth Trust Medal and in the case of PC Carss, the Silver Medal of the Scouting Association for Bravery. Constables of Courage, without doubt.

ORGANISATIONS & LEISURE
TYNEMOUTH VOLUNTEER LIFE BRIGADE

At around 4 pm on the evening of 24th November 1864 the evening begins to draw in with heavy rain. An east-south easterly gale starts to blow and a wild night threatens. As the tide is half-spent with a high sea, a small schooner runs aground on the rocks beneath the Spanish Battery. Rocket gear is taken down to the rocks to land the crew by breeches buoy, but the crew is already thought to be safe thanks to the Shields lifeboat and so the gear is returned to the store. The men are still aboard. The schooner is called *Friendship*.

Meanwhile, as darkness gathered, the Glasgow to London Passenger steamship *Stanley* sailed into the Tyne to take shelter from the storm, however the vessel approaches too far to the north to be successful and is swept into a stream of broken water from which she failed to recover and is soon dashed onto the tip of the Spanish Battery Rocks – the infamous Black Middens. As the doomed ship launches two distress rockets, the Tynemouth lifeboat; *Constance* put to sea in an attempt to rescue the crew and passengers. As an effort was made to land some of the *SS Stanley's* passengers in one of her boats, it was capsized by a heavy wave, drowning all the occupants within a few yards of the shore.

At this time, the coastguard consisted only of four men (two of whom were pensioners), and despite their desperate efforts using a breeches buoy, the lines became tangled, and all attempts to save the passengers and crew were in vain. Between the two vessels, a total of 34 lives perished in the water within sight of hundreds of spectators. The gales continued into the following day, and the very next evening the brig *Martin Luther* was lost with all hands on the South Pier. Only days later on 28th November the barques *Reaper* and *Amy Robsart* were also wrecked and stranded on the Black Midden rocks, their crews fortunately saved by the lifeboat.

The wreck of the Steamer SS Stanley on the Black Middens in 1864.

These disastrous occurrences led to a suggestion for the formation of a Volunteer Life Brigade, conceived by a Mr John Morrison, a young rifle volunteer officer who was present during that fateful night and was stirred to ensure that the consequences of such disasters should never occur again.

He was of the opinion that the tragic loss of life may have been lessened if the coastguard had been able to draw on a trained reserve force to assist them in their endeavours, rather than relying on the well-intentioned but disorganised efforts of would-be rescuers. On 5th December 1864, along with two willing colleagues, Mr John Foster Spence and Mr Joseph Spence, a public meeting was arranged at North Shields Town Hall, where it was resolved to form a brigade of volunteers whose self-imposed duty should be render skilled assistance to the coastguard. It was proposed that the brigade would consist of four companies of thirty men, each led by a captain and within a short space of time, over 140 men from all classes willingly came forward as volunteers. Tynemouth Volunteer Life Brigade had now been formed.

The first drill of the Brigade was held on 11th February 1865 with a muster of 83 members, and the first callout of the service was on 19th March 1865 during a heavy gale when the coal-laden brig *Burton* was driven onto rocks and rolled over onto her side at the end of the North Pier. The brigadesmen fired a rocket line over the ship, but managed to liberate just one survivor; a Mr George Hazell who was subsequently rescued by the Tynemouth Lifeboat *Constance*.

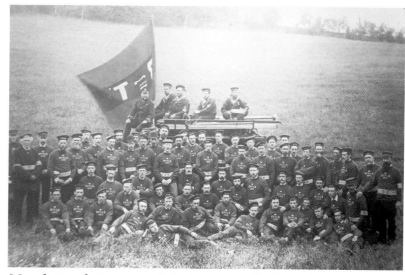

Members of Tynemouth Volunteer Life Brigade, c. 1900.

It was not until 8th February 1870 that the Brigade's endeavours were crowned with success after saving three men from the brigantine *Susannah,* which had been wrecked on the Spanish Battery rocks, which was followed only hours later when a schooner, *Light of Heaven* drifted behind the North Pier. Its crew of five was safely rescued with the use of rocket apparatus in less than sixteen minutes, following which the vessel quickly broke up in heavy seas.

Sadly, the first casualty of the Brigade occurred on 17th December 1872, when Robert Thirlway Arkley was washed away and drowned, during a rescue attempt after the barque *Consul* was driven onto the pier and wrecked in heavy seas. This is the only loss of life suffered by the TVLB in its history.

When the Board of Trade's approval and assistance had been enlisted, they were so impressed with the performance of the Tynemouth men, that they circulated the rules of TVLB to every coastguard station in the country, to be used as the basis of similar organisations around the UK coastline.

The TVLB itself is a wholly self-organised and financed service using the latest rescue and communications equipment, all of which is paid for by voluntary public donations. Since the formation of the brigade in 1864, they still serve the same purpose as their predecessors – The saving of life from the sea. Since that date, they have responded to thousands of callouts and saved many lives. The members of Tynemouth Volunteer Life Brigade are trained to high standards and continue to function as a voluntary coastal search and rescue service, working closely with HM Coastguard and the local RNLI Lifeboats.

The purpose-built Watch House, originally built in 1887, overlooks the mouth of the River Tyne and the team is based here. As guardians of one of the most important parts of Tynemouth's heritage, the committee has registered the Watch House as a national museum which is open to the public. The museum contains a fascinating collection of unique and unusual artifacts and relics, as well as a superb written and pictorial history of the brigade's existence.

To the left of the photo: Tynemouth Volunteer Life Brigade Watch House in 1899.

TYNEMOUTH LIFEBOAT

The mouth of the River Tyne has always played a very important part in the history of lifeboats which itself is a complicated subject area. The Tyne Lifeboat Society however, first established a station in 1790 with the lifeboat *Original*, the first in the world to be built (although in 1786 a coble had been converted into a life-saving vessel and was based at Bamburgh).

When a Lifeboat service had been firmly established at Tynemouth, this was not without a cost to human life. The first recorded tragedy struck on 4th December 1846 when the Tyne Lifeboat *Providence* capsized whilst on service to the brig *Betsy* with the loss of 20 of her crew.

Eventually, the first Tynemouth lifeboat house was constructed and established in 1862 at a cost of £380. In 1884, improvements were made to the slipway which was extended to include levelling of the rocks before further work was carried out in 1897 to include widening and further lengthening of the slipway. By 1905, the station closed and an experimental motor lifeboat was brought in for trials under the supervision of a Lt. H.E. Burton RE.

It should be noted that the nearby Tynemouth Volunteer Life Brigade is also very active in this area, specialising in rescues from the shore. Until 1905 when the RNLI number two lifeboat station closed several men were members of both organisations. The Tyne Lifeboat Society however remained independent of the TVLB,

In 1919 the old lifeboat house which stood at Priors Haven was sold to Tynemouth Sailing Club for £130. In April 1941, during the Second World War, the lifeboat station was destroyed by enemy action but was re-opened six months later.

On 16th September 1962, the Duchess of Northumberland unveiled a stained glass window in the Seamen's Chapel of Christ Church, North Shields, to commemorate the Centenary of the Tynemouth lifeboat station. The window, which was donated by the coxswain and crew, incorporated a picture of the first lifeboat named *Original* which was built on Tyneside. In June 1980, a new lifeboat *George and Olive Turner* was named by the Duchess of Northumberland.

In February 1997, construction work was completed on a new building to provide the station with improved crew facilities. Also constructed was a small extension to the rear of the existing boathouse in order to provide housing for a B class lifeboat and launching tractor coupled in-line.

Tynemouth Lifeboat – The Spirit of Northumberland.

The 7th October 1998 saw an incident when the Tynemouth 'D' class lifeboat capsized in surf whilst on service. Fortunately there were no injuries to crew or damage to the ILB. Improved boarding facilities were completed in September 2004 at a cost of £20,151. Tynemouth RNLI lifeboat station currently operates two lifeboats: A 'D' class inshore lifeboat called *Mark Noble* and a Severn class all-weather lifeboat called *Spirit of Northumberland*.

Since its inception, the organisation has carried out many rescue missions and many achievements have been recorded and recognised with various awards. Over the years, twenty-two Medals have been awarded (2 Gold, 15 Silver and 5 Bronze) for acts of bravery, courage and heroism. The RNLI make awards to anyone who merits them, not just RNLI crews.

The table below shows some of the bravery awards given by the RNLI for those notable and accomplished missions by the various crews of Tynemouth Lifeboat and other related individuals;

1828 (1st December): Henry Strachan, a Pilot rescued a crew of five who had capsized in the River Tyne at Newcastle in a Custom House boat. He was awarded the RNLI Silver Medal.

1830 (16th September): William Tully, a Pilot rescued the Master and two seamen from the sloop *Friendship* wrecked off Spanish Battery, near Shields Harbour. He was awarded the RNLI Silver Medal.

1839 (12th March): T. Thorp, storekeeper of the rockets, rescued the Master and 10 seamen of the ship *Progress* that was stranded on 12th March 1839. He was awarded the RNLI Silver Medal.

1843 (23rd January): John Cunningham rescued an apprentice by rocket line from the *Constantia* which was wrecked at Tynemouth. He was awarded the RNLI Silver Medal.

1848: William Wheeler, a Pilot saved four of the crew of the brig *Percy* which had been wrecked on the rocks under Tynemouth Castle. In 1851 he also saved one crewman from the Danish Brig *Margaretta* which capsized in the River Thames. He was awarded the RNLI Silver Medal.

1864 (24th November): Lawrence Byrne, a Coastguard, showed gallantry and perseverance when the schooner *Friendship* and the steamer *Stanley* found themselves in difficulties in gale force winds off Tynemouth Point. Both vessels were driven onto the rocks with waves breaking over them. Mr Byrne set up rocket apparatus on the shore and managed to establish contact with the steamer and saved 38 people. In a simultaneous attempt by the lifeboat *Constance*, four of her crew were washed out and two, James Grant and Edmund Robson, were drowned. Lawrence Byrne was awarded the RNLI Silver Medal.

1872 (17th December): Members of the TVLB and coastguards were attempting to rescue the crew of the barque *Consul* which was attempting to enter the Tyne in severe weather. The barque struck a pier and within 15 minutes was reduced to matchwood. The rescuers on the pier managed to save some of her crew, but during the attempt it was believed that one rescuer had been washed away by the sea. A subsequent search found the body of Robert Thirlway Arkley. Mr Arkley, a customs officer, was not only a member of the TVLB but also an RNLI crew member.

1886 (3rd June): James Gilbert, coxswain of the Tynemouth Lifeboat since 1862, was awarded the RNLI Silver Medal in recognition of his long and valuable services to the lifeboat. He was given a second award in November 1898 on his retirement.

1913 (11th January): Silver Medals were awarded to Captain H.E. Burton, Coxswain Robert Smith (and Coxswain Anthony Nixon, Cambois lifeboat) for the part they played in rescuing the crew of the *Dunelm*, wrecked off Blyth. The Blyth lifeboat was unable to get out of the harbour and the Tynemouth lifeboat arrived just as the last man was being rescued by the rocket apparatus.

1914 (30th October - 1st November): Captain H.E. Burton and Coxswain Robert Smith, Second Coxswain James Brownlee and Lt Basil Hall, Lifeboat Inspector, rescued the last 50 survivors from the hospital ship *Rohilla* which had ran aground on a dangerous reef during a gale at Saltwick Nab. The lifeboat battled 45 miles down an unlit coast against the gale and took nine hours to reach the wreck near Whitby. As a result, the following were awarded the RNLI Gold Medal: Coxswain Thomas Langlands of the Whitby Lifeboat and Captain Herbert Edgar Burton and Coxswain Robert Smith, both of the Tynemouth Lifeboat, were awarded the RNLI Gold Medal. The RNLI Silver Medal was awarded to, Commander Basil Hall, RN, District Inspector of Lifeboats, who was in the Tynemouth Lifeboat, Henry Eglon, Second Coxswain of the Whitby Lifeboat, James S. Brownlee, Second Coxswain of the Tynemouth Lifeboat, and George Peart, a bricklayer, who had rushed into the sea to help survivors coming ashore.

1916 (19th - 21st November): Coxswain Robert Smith and Second Coxswain James Brownlee rescued 16 people, in a dangerous operation, from the steamship *Muristan* after she ran ashore at Blyth. They were each awarded their second RNLI Silver Medal.

1916 (19th November): The crew and passengers (118 in total) were rescued from the steamship *Bessheim*. HM the King of Norway later awarded a Silver Cup to the coxswain and Silver Medals to the crew in recognition of this. Medals were also awarded to the crew of the private lifeboat *Tom Perry*.

1926 (8th August): Ordinary Seaman Michael Campbell RNVR rescued a man who had been thrown into the river when his boat capsized near the coble landing.

1940 (8th December): Edward Selby Davidson, Honorary Secretary of the Tynemouth Branch, and Coxswain George Lisle assisted in the rescue of 22 of the crew of the Norwegian motor vessel *Oslo Fjord* which ran ashore south of the Tyne in a strong north-north-easterly wind. They were each awarded the RNLI Bronze Medal.

1974 (10th March): Trevor Fryer and Frederick Arkley assisted with the rescue of a crew of three men and a boy from the tug *Northsider* which had been driven onto the Black Midden Rocks in a strong easterly wind and a rough sea whilst assisting the oil exploration ship *Oregis* which had been grounded on rocks at Freestone Point near the Black Middens. They were each awarded the RNLI Bronze Medal.

1982 (11th April): Helmsman Trevor Fryer assisted in the rescue of nine people from the vessel 'Blue Fin' in a strong northerly wind and rough breaking seas.

1986 (15th April): Coxswain John Hogg assisted in the rescue of a crew of three from the fishing vessel *La Morlaye* in an east-south-easterly gale and heavy breaking seas. He was awarded the RNLI Silver Medal.

1998 (3rd April): Coxwain Martin Kenny and crew members Edwin Chapple, Geoffrey Cowan, Kevin Mole and Michael Nugent for the service to the yacht *Signature* were presented with a letter of thanks from the Chairman.

POLICING IN TYNEMOUTH

Both residents and visitors have commented on the sandstone façade to be found at the foot of Front Street, representing the coat of arms of the former Borough of Tynemouth. Significantly, it was restored some years ago by John Jackson, a former policeman and stonemason, as it came from the old police station in Oxford Street, which was closed in the 1920s and demolished in the 1950s to make way for new housing.

Tynemouth Village was situated too far from the Saville Street Police Headquarters to be adequately policed so the Oxford Street station was built shortly after the formation of Tynemouth Borough Police in 1850. The station was equipped with suitable offices and cells, and the rear yard was used for drill and stabling purposes, as transport was confined to horseback or size 10 boots! The residents of the village began to enjoy a hitherto unknown level of policing, for until then, Parish Constables or Watchmen appointed by local businessmen, justices of the Peace and Parish officials were the only means of protection afforded, and they fell woefully short of necessity. The duties of these early stalwarts included patrolling the streets and narrow alleys both day and night, but especially the latter, dealing with whatever lawbreaking activities they encountered. As most of them were poorly paid and often in other employment, the standard of policing was predictably low, with many a 'Blind Eye' being turned if an element of danger was threatened.

Primitive street lighting maintenance was the province of the watchman, as well as sewage and the clearing of litter. Little wonder the job was not a popular one! With the passing of the Municipal Corporations Act of 1835, towns and cities, (depending on their population size) were bound to form organised, disciplined and controlled police forces. Tynemouth fell into this category, but delayed forming such a force until 1st January 1850, probably because the Charter of Incorporation giving

North Shields Police Uniform, 1840-50.

County Borough status was not instituted until 1849. Meanwhile, the town of North Shields had employed 10 fully uniformed men to patrol the main areas and waterfront since 1828.

On its formation, Tynemouth Borough Police was under the command of Robert Mitchell, a Superintendent from the Metropolitan Police which had been in successful operation since 1829. The Tynemouth force was increased numerically and formed into three divisions: Central (Saville Street), West End (Lawson Street) and Tynemouth (Oxford Street). Chief Constable Blackburn introduced police boxes in 1929, and the first vehicle, an Alvis, was bought in 1933. As these innovations usefully addressed the need for better communications, the two outlying stations were decommissioned and the force operated from the central police station on Saville Street. The borough was initially divided into 12 'beats', but by the time of the 1969 amalgamation these had increased to 22 and were coupled into areas when in 1965 the 'Panda' car system was introduced.

TYNEMOUTH TRAMWAYS

Tynemouth and District Tramways Company operated from a depot in Suez Street, North Shields on the site of what was later to become Unicorn House. In 1879, the company received permission to build a horse tramway from Camden Street, North Shields, to Grand Parade, Tynemouth, a

The Old Steam Trams were relegated to a yard at Tynemouth and are waiting here in 1890 to be broken up and scrapped.

distance of just over 2.5 miles. The line and cars were inspected on 29th June 1880 and the route was opened the next day however the venture failed and they went bankrupt the following year (1881).

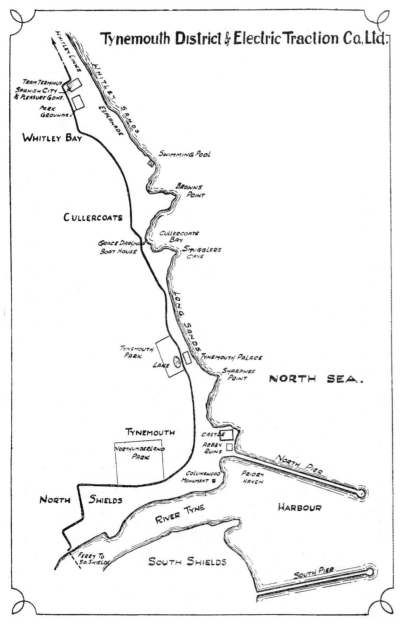

In 1882 North Shields and District Tramways Company was set up and took over the system. By 1884 the company had introduced a total of five steam trams on the route and extended the line from Camden Street as far as Prudhoe Street, however this company also failed and by 1886 had become bankrupt. Their line was adopted and reopened in 1890 by North Shields & Tynemouth District Tramways Limited, which in 1899 was taken over by the British Electric Traction Company who renamed the business 'The Tynemouth and District Electric Traction Company'. This takeover saw a modernisation of the fleet with work commencing on the electrification of the system in 1900.

On 1st March 1901, electric trams were introduced with a new tramway system running from the New Quay at North Shields, terminating outside the Victoria Hotel in Whitley. The first services ran on 18th March 1901. This line was extended in 1904 from the Victoria Hotel to the Bandstand on Whitley Links.

Electric Power was supplied by the new Tynemouth Corporation Power Station, which was situated on Tanners Bank. Towards the end of the tramway's life the ten minute service was run alternatively with buses. These were considered to be the future transport and the last tram ran from the New Quay on the evening of 4th August 1931.

The tram route ran as follows: New Quay, Borough Bank, Saville Street, Howard Street, Norfolk Street, Albion Road, Tynemouth Road, Allendale Place, Percy Park Road, Grand Parade, Beverley Terrace, John Street, Whitley Road, Park Avenue, Park Road, Marine Avenue, The Links (Bandstand).

Right: The Tram Terminus at the New Quay, North Shields.

The Tram Terminus at the Bandstand on Whitley Links.

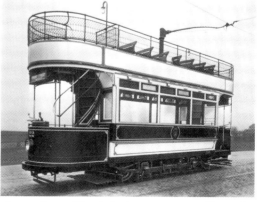

A modern Electric tramcar on Grand Parade, belonging to the Tynemouth and District Electric Traction Company.

The Tynemouth & District Electric Traction Co., Ltd.

Operate Trams and Buses throughout the district as shown on map opposite.

TRAMS leave Whitley Bay every few minutes for North Shields and Ferries to South Shields. BUSES run to Blyth and Wallsend at frequent intervals. (Red marked Tynemouth Tramways.)

SPECIAL TRAMS may be booked at reasonable charges and BUSES may be hired for private parties, special trips, outings, etc.

For terms and particulars apply to
TYNEMOUTH TRAMWAYS,
JOHN STREET, CULLERCOATS.
'Phone – Whitley Bay 17.

J. A. SOMERVILLE,
Manager.

THE PRIORY MOTOR COACH COMPANY

The Priory Motor Coach Company was founded and established in 1929 at North Shields by a man called George Chapman. Coaches were garaged at premises situated at Queen Street, North Shields, however the office and operating centre was based at George's home which was located at No 33 Waterloo Place. This house once displayed a stained glass fanlight above the front door depicting Tynemouth Priory which may have given rise to the choice of name. In 2014, only the word 'Priory' is evident above the door. In later years, the business moved to a shop situated at No 59 Church Way, North Shields where it has remained to the present day.

The company survived throughout the Second World War and by the late 1940s, Priory were running over 40 coaches on a private hire basis as well as operating tours and excursions throughout the North of England. Many of the coaches in those days were built to a maximum of 33 seats and were liveried in dark green and cream, before becoming two-tone green in 1969.

Early Priory Coaches at the Queen Street Garage, North Shields, c. 1938.

George Chapman died during the mid 1950s and his widow, Mary continued to run the business in conjunction with the then transport manager, Jack Watson. In 1965, the business was eventually sold and came into the hands of a Selby Blenkinsop, who with a consortium also owned Team Valley Dairies at Gateshead, however Jack Watson continued to run the company on their behalf. During this time, a number of changes took place within the company, and new split-level garage premises were acquired at Northumberland Street, North Shields with workshop facilities on the lower level. The same year, a man called Stuart Lee took up employment with Priory Coaches as a fitter and remained with the company for a number of years.

In 1973, Jack Watson died, as a result of which Stuart took over as Transport Manager, and in later years he purchased shares in the company along with other employees. Over the years, the fleet was reduced in size, and in 2001, the company operated just 10 coaches, and it was during this year that Stuart retired from the business, selling out the company to a Mr Jed Patrick. Priory Coaches are still well known in the area with their redesigned and distinctive modern livery, however their success story still continues.

TYNEMOUTH GOLF CLUB

Spital Dene generally comprises the area which forms part of the present golf course and runs south across King Edward Road (a section of which once bore the macabre name of 'Cut-Throat Lane'), to Northumberland Park, and incorporates part of the stream known as the 'Pow Burn'. This land formed part of the Duke of Northumberland's estate. Soon after the turn of the 1900s, it was suggested that the laying out of a golf course at Spital Dene had some potential. The land contours here would provide an ideal course and as a result, significant interest was soon generated. By 1913, Tynemouth Golf Course had been firmly established and was laid out on part of these lands adjacent to the area which was known as Spital Dene Farm. The old farmhouse along with some of the former outbuildings still exist and over the years have been converted for a variety of purposes including staff accommodation and the provision of basic facilities and amenities for members and players. The first course here was designed by a renowned Scottish golfer and course architect – Mr Willie Park Jnr, and consisted of just 15 holes, so in order to make up a full 18-hole round, the holes numbered 1 to 3 were played again as the 16th, 17th and 18th, however this often led to some congestion on the tees. As a result, it was decided that

efforts should be made to try and acquire some of the adjacent farmland in an effort to extend the course and make up the three 'missing' holes. These plans however were interrupted with the outbreak of the Great War of 1914-18, because part of the war effort meant that it was necessary to utilise the land occupied by the course to be let out for grazing; a necessary inconvenience, however this avoided the need to plough up the newly-laid fairways. As a small measure of compensation, the War Department paid £20 per year to the club which brought in a small but helpful additional revenue. At the end of the Great War, the club resumed its plans to try and acquire more land to extend the course with the inclusion of new 16th, 17th and 18th holes. For a number of years, none of the neighbouring tenant farmers were willing to release any of their land to cater for this, however in 1936 following the death of one of the farmers, the club managed to negotiate the sale of additional land to secure an extra 10 acre field which enabled the appropriate course extension to go ahead as planned.

The former outbuildings of Spital Dene Farm are now occupied by Tynemouth Golf Club.

In 1938, the new and extended course was redesigned by Mr James Braid, another renowned Scottish golfer, however due to the outbreak of the Second World War a number of legal delays were encountered and the new field was once again requisitioned for agricultural purposes as a result of the war effort. It was fortunate however that the club managed to negotiate with the authorities to enable the site to be used for pasture and grazing, thus avoiding the need to plough up the entire land for crops. This necessary interruption once again meant that the members had to share the existing fairways with cattle and sheep and it was not until 1952, that the club was able to open up with the new and complete 18-hole course.

Another major reconstruction of the course came in 1957/58 when a further 15-acre field on the northwest boundary became available. Holes on the northern section of the course were extended and re-sited to form the basic layout which still exists to this day. Many other improvements have been made to the course since the 1950s which have included the planting of shrubs and trees and the redesign of some bunkers, as a result of which, Tynemouth is considered to be one of the most attractive parkland courses in the North East of England.

Although Spital Dene farm buildings have served the club well for a number of years a proposal was submitted in the mid 1930s for the erection of a new purpose-built clubhouse. Some delays were encountered over the lease and the raising of sufficient finance, however the matter was eventually resolved and building work commenced.

The new clubhouse, situated adjacent to Preston Avenue, opened in January 1940 but immediately, a number of wartime restrictions began to affect its smooth running due to utility interruptions, blackouts, rationing and early closures etc. Apparently, at one stage, only members were permitted service in the clubhouse and were limited to one half measure of whisky.

Records indicate that during the early days of the golf club, green fees amounted to two shillings per day or £1 for a 4-week ticket and play was not actually permitted on Sundays until October 1918.

In 2013, Tynemouth Golf Club celebrated 100 years of existence over which time, a number of improvements have been made to the course and the clubhouse building, which includes enclosure of the original north-facing verandahs. The single-storey design however remains basically unchanged.

TYNEMOUTH ROWING CLUB

Tynemouth Rowing Club was formed in 1867 and since then has carried on a proud tradition of rowing. The club owns a number of boats, some of which are sleek and light, designed for racing whilst others are heavier and stronger and are more suited for the coastal conditions at Tynemouth. The clubhouse is situated in a sheltered cove at Priors Haven, Tynemouth at the point where the river Tyne meets the North Sea. Facilities include a bar and social area, which includes ladies and gents toilets and showers. There is also a small gym which includes rowing machines for dry training sessions. When conditions are not favourable for rowing, the club offer options for dry-land training, such as circuits and beach workouts etc.

Members of Tynemouth Rowing Club, pre-1900.

TYNEMOUTH AMATEUR SWIMMING CLUB

Records indicate that a Swimming Club had been formed at Tynemouth in 1859 but it appears to have been disbanded eight years later in June 1867. On 10th August 1875, the organisation was reinstated under the name of Tynemouth Amateur Swimming Club and has since undergone a long tradition of promoting swimming in the area. The Founder Member was a Mr John William Moore, who owned a printing works in Charlotte Street, North Shields. He was a keen swimmer who taught many thousands of people how to swim.

Mr John W. Moore – Founder.

In 1888, the club had a purpose built 'Bathing House' which was erected on the South Slope of Tynemouth Pier and was used for a number of years until it was washed away during a gale in the Spring of 1915. In 1907, the club applied to the local council to use a small open air, salt water reservoir situated in Hawkey's Lane for which permission was granted. The reservoir however was small and measured only 60 foot square at a depth of just 5 feet with sloping sides. Although once very popular, it was inadequate to sustain a large numbers of swimmers. As a result, additional land was secured and on 30th June 1909, a brand new, purpose built open air salt water swimming bath was opened on the same site. Extended to a size of 100 foot long by 40 foot wide, the management of the baths was handed over to the club, under a body of trustees. The new bath included covered stands capable of accommodating up to 600 spectators.

The popularity of the club soon increased and once had a total membership of 1,358.

Tynemouth ASC members, c. 1910.

The salt water was replaced with a fresh water supply in 1946. In 1971 the club moved from the outdoor baths to its present site at Tynemouth Indoor Pool, and continues its long tradition of providing swimming excellence for many people of the local area.

Rare film footage from a Tynemouth Amateur Swimming Clubs gala held in 1901 just off Tynemouth North Pier is available to view on the internet by typing the following link into your browser: http://youtube/VWz—7FEaV8.

A Swimming Gala held at Hawkey's Lane Swimming Baths around 1910.

PERCY PARK RUGBY FOOTBALL CLUB

Percy Park Rugby Football Club was founded in 1872 by J. Stanley Todd, who lived with his Uncle in the large terraced houses at No 60 Percy Park, Tynemouth. The team originally played in a field behind his home and hence, the name of the club was derived from this street. When the fields behind Percy Park were taken over for gardens in 1879, the club moved on and played on Collingwood Monument fields, overlooking the harbour. By 1880 Percy Park Football Club became one of the six founder members of the Northumberland RFU. The other founder members being the Northumberland Football Club, the (original) Borough of Tynemouth Football Club, the Northern Football Club, the (original) Gosforth Football Club and the Tynedale Football Club. In 1881, the team had moved and was playing on Dolphin Field, however this was only available on Saturday afternoons. The players had to erect goal posts before the game and then take them down afterwards and they were stored in the yard of the nearby Dolphin Inn.

Mr J. Stanley Todd, founder of Percy Park Rugby Football Club.

Mr Dunn, the landlord of the Inn, was a keen supporter and allowed his premises to be used for changing purposes. Meetings at this time were held in 'Medley's' in Nile Street and later in the decade the committee met for a brief period at the Albion Inn and then for many years at 'Raynors' also in Nile Street and just ten years after formation of the club, its membership in 1882 had reached 100.

By 1884, the club was playing at Hunt Hill, Hawkeys Lane which was known as the Old Earl Percy Field and was to the south of Preston Cemetery. It was said that the first team players had the privilege of using a bedroom in one of the cottages near the gate as a dressing room, however they had to perform their ablutions in a bucket in the yard. The third and fourth teams, however, had to be content with hanging their coats on the Cemetery wall.

The site of Appleby Park became a new venue for the team in 1887, however an old disused mine shaft collapsed under the field leaving a chasm where hundreds of tons of rubble were used as infill.

The field was subsequently taken over and occupied by North Shields AFC. After a number of playing venues and moves during the early years of the club, a final move was made in 1896 to a new venue on Preston Avenue where the team have been situated ever since. In 1889, the club changed their strip from black jerseys and blue knickerbockers to familiar black and white hoops.

The club badge, originally a red star was changed in 1928, and incorporated the Percy Lion which was adopted as the new club emblem. Following the Second World War, the club was financially stable and so in 1949 they purchased their present ground for the sum of £3,000. Amongst the tributes a memorial tablet was unveiled in memory of those players who had made the ultimate sacrifice for King and Country.

In 1955 a new clubhouse was built and was opened by the Duke of Northumberland. The same year, negotiations began to lease a second playing area on an area locally known as 'Harbottles Field'.

A new concrete stand was built in 1983 replacing an earlier wooden framework which burned down and further construction work in 1998 saw the building of a new clubhouse equipped with modern facilities. Over the years which followed, various other modernisations and improvements have been carried out to the clubhouse and grounds as Percy Park RFC steadily progress into the future.

TYNEMOUTH PRIORY THEATRE

Tynemouth Priory Theatre club was formed in 1946 by Miss Ria Thompson. Forty founder members signed up and paid a membership fee of 10/6d (52p). The first full length production was *Blithe Spirit* by Noel Coward and was performed in Holy Saviours Parish Hall which for a time became the club's temporary home. A shortage of venues and a lack of funds meant that for many years the Priory did not have a home of its own, and each time the Parish Hall was hired, it meant setting up all the seats and lighting and transferring all the scenery on a truck from the rehearsal rooms in order to build the set overnight. Membership gradually increased, and by 1951/52, the theatre membership stood at 375.

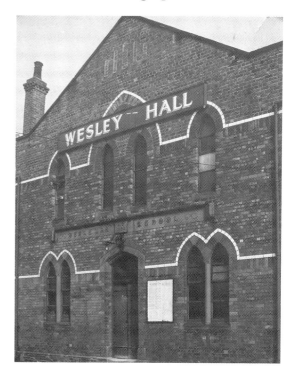

After many successful performances over the years, the club prospered and found a more permanent home when the former Wesleyan Chapel and School (built 1882) in Percy Street was purchased in 1971. The members then set about transforming it into a traditional theatre, which entailed significant alteration work, including changes to the outside of the building. The arched Chapel windows were bricked up and sealed, and the external walls rendered, however the original stone date plaque was left intact above the front door and the former Chapel is now only recognisable by its frontal profile.

When conversion work was complete in 1972, the team gradually built up to five productions a year plus pantomimes and occasional interims and in 1976/77 the theatre hosted its first drama festival, and sadly, three years later in 1980, the founder, Ria Thompson died. As testimony to Ria, and its founder members, it is with a source of great pride that the organisation now own their own theatre. Many visitors have often described it as a little jewel. Over the years many building improvements have been carried out and refurbishment work has ensured the comfort of all the patrons whilst affording good facilities for the members. The main focus of activity is performing plays within the theatre, however the social side is regarded as being equally important.

There are regular club nights when members put on play-readings, mini-play performances, quiz nights and the like. Coffee is served every Saturday morning when members meet to chat, discuss and plan various social activities. Play-readings are a regular occurrence too, usually before any formal auditions. Everything within the theatre, whether associated with productions, rehearsals, stage management,

wardrobes, props or maintenance is carried out by the members. Sets, backdrops and costumes are all made and stored in-house.

The theatre relies on ticket sales and raffles, and along with its own Script Library, income is also generated by hiring out scenery cloths, sets and furniture to other theatre groups. During the main theatre season, five main productions are scheduled. Each play is performed over six nights from Monday to Saturday. During the winter season, pantomimes run throughout January, usually with twelve performances which include Saturday Matinees.

Also available from Summerhill Books

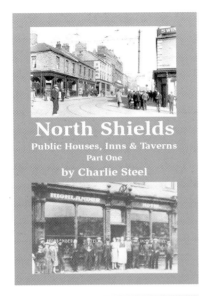

North Shields
Public Houses, Inns & Taverns
Part One
by Charlie Steel

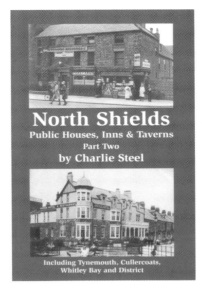

North Shields
Public Houses, Inns & Taverns
Part Two
by Charlie Steel

Including Tynemouth, Cullercoats,
Whitley Bay and District

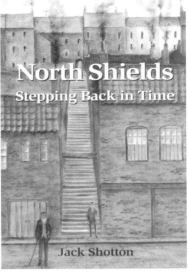

North Shields
Stepping Back in Time

Jack Shotton

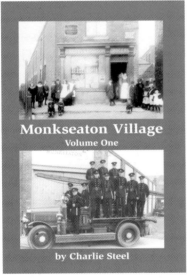

Monkseaton Village
Volume One

by Charlie Steel

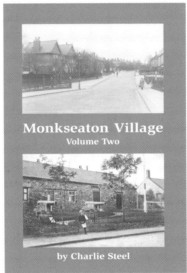

Monkseaton Village
Volume Two

by Charlie Steel

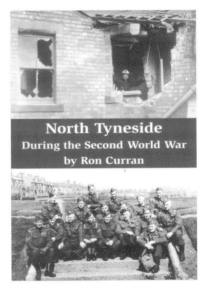

North Tyneside
During the Second World War
by Ron Curran

OFFBEAT
Memories of Tynemouth Borough Police
and the communities it served
North Shields, Tynemouth & Cullercoats

by Ken Banks

**Deaths, Disasters &
Dastardly Deeds**
in the North East
by Lorna Windham

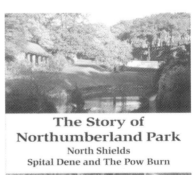

**The Story of
Northumberland Park**
North Shields
Spital Dene and The Pow Burn

Mike N. Coates

Summerhill Books publishes North East local history books. To receive a catalogue of
our titles send a stamped addressed envelope to: Summerhill Books, PO Box 1210,
Newcastle-upon-Tyne NE99 4AH   or email: summerhillbooks@yahoo.co.uk

or visit our website to view our full range of books: **www.summerhillbooks.co.uk**